step up to
Wordpower

Carolyn Kewley and Angela Lee for

Adult Literacy & Basic Skills Unit

BBC BOOKS

Dear Reader

This book is about the skills involved in communicating with other people. It's about how to get across or receive information and ideas through reading, writing, talking and listening. It also looks at the way messages are put over through pictures (graphics) and at how new technology is affecting communication in our lives.

Each section of the book will remind you that, when reading, writing, talking or listening, you need to be aware of *who* you are communicating with (**audience**) and the *reason* for doing so (**purpose**). This awareness is what will put power into your communication skills.

So if you are keen to improve the way you communicate with others, whether at home, at work or when studying, we hope this book will help you check out the skills you already own, open up new pathways and allow you to *Step Up to Wordpower*.

Carolyn Kewley and Angela Lee

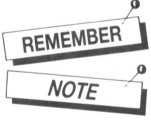 **These symbols have been used to help you as you work through the book:**

 Key points to think about.

 Something to do or think about as you are working through a section.

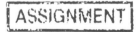 This pulls all the main points in a section together.

 Suggestions for work as a follow-up to the section.

Books A few suggestions for books you may like to buy or borrow. (You can always find out more about most topics at your local library.)

Contents

Finding the right words   4

Dictionaries and wordfinders   7

1. Writing

Things that matter in writing   10

Getting started with writing   25

Editing and proofreading   30

Letters and letter writing   34

Forms and form-filling   45

Notes   50

Personal writing   53

2. Reading

Reading skills   56

Reading beyond the words   62

Reading to learn   65

Reading for pleasure   68

3. Talking and listening

Talking and listening skills   70

Using the telephone   78

Communication in groups   84

Interviews   87

Communicating with graphics   89

Communication and IT   93

Finding the right words

Step Up to Wordpower is all about the way we use words.

This section is about *finding the right words*, which means:

- saying exactly what you mean . . .

but also

- having some thought for your reader/listener

When we communicate with words, we usually want the other person

- to understand us and get the message
- be interested and take notice
- feel comfortable with our tone/style

However, sometimes we don't get it right and our reader/listener will suffer . . .

> *I wonder why she always uses such long words*

> *I think it means we don't need to fill in section B*

> *I've read it 4 times and I still don't know what it means*

> *She goes on and on and bores everyone around her*

> *He used lots of abbreviations like C.T.R.B. and I didn't like to stop him to ask what they meant*

. . . and this could lead to someone

- not taking you or your ideas seriously
- not giving you the job
- not giving you a pass mark in a test or exam
- not publishing your work
- not giving you the information you needed
- not wanting to talk to you

Have you ever heard or read something which:

had too many complicated words ☐

didn't really use the best words ☐

was unclear in meaning ☐

was too long and wordy ☐

used too many abbreviations ☐

didn't sound right for the purpose ☐

You might like to match these to the following examples.

Scintillate, Scintillate,
Diminutive asteroid.
(TWINKLE, TWINKLE,
LITTLE STAR)

Personally, if you ask my opinion, I think,
and it's only my view you understand,
that if I were you, I think . . .

P.M. has got G.R.I.S.T.
Funding for a N.A.F.E. A.B.E.
event organised by
N.C.F.E./A.L.B.S.U.

Dear Sir,
I'd love to work for your firm 'cos it'd be really great being able to paint all day. I get a real buzz out of decorating and if you could see the way I . . . . .

She told her that she wanted to but she thought she had told her that it was . . .

It was good and nice and I like it a lot.

The English language is rich in words. Unfortunately, it is not always used in the best way.

Some people like to use the longest and the most complicated words whenever they can to *impress* others,

(even when *simple* language would be more impressive).

Other people lack power in their writing or speaking because they don't make good use of all the words available to them,

(often because they aren't sure how to spell them or because they don't know where to find them).

It really is a question of getting the right balance.

☑ **YES,** there are times when communication needs to use *technical* or *complicated* language.
⎫ *legal documents,*
⎬ *technical reports/discussion,*
⎭ *medical terms.*

☑ **YES,** there are times when communication should be as *short* and *simple* as possible.
⎫ *information on forms,*
⎬ *memos,*
⎭ *messages.*

So how can you tell when you've got the right balance?

You are more likely to get it right when you've thought about:

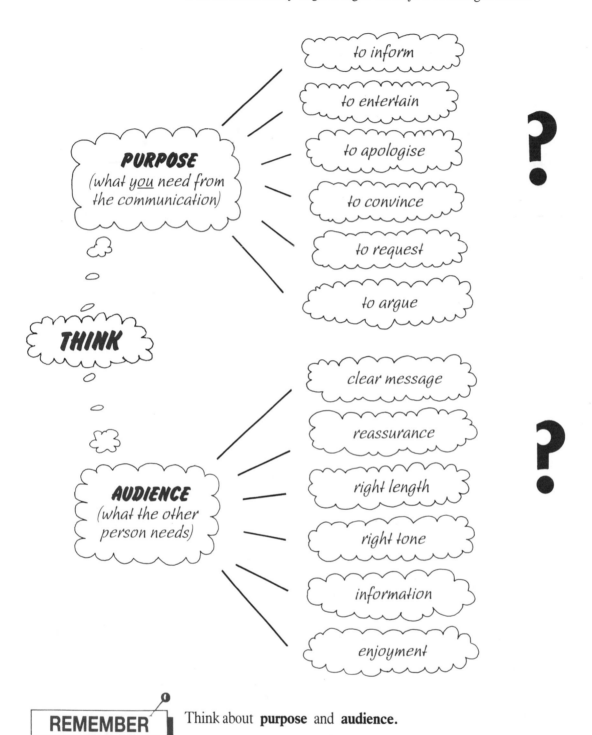

REMEMBER

Think about **purpose** and **audience**.

This is the basis for all good communication.

We will be reminding you of this as you work through the other sections in this book.

Dictionaries and wordfinders

A good dictionary can tell you many things about words.

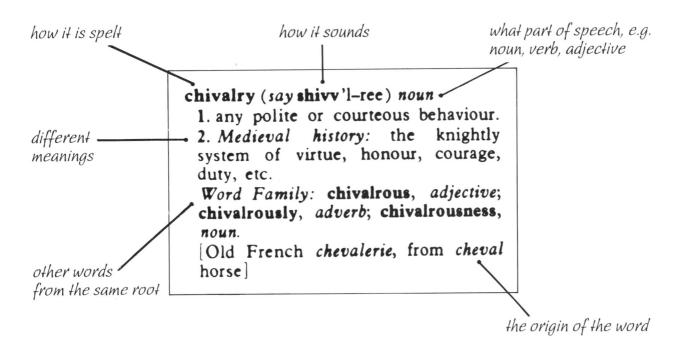

how it is spelt

how it sounds

what part of speech, e.g. noun, verb, adjective

different meanings

other words from the same root

the origin of the word

chivalry (*say* **shivv**'l–ree) *noun*
1. any polite or courteous behaviour.
2. *Medieval history:* the knightly system of virtue, honour, courage, duty, etc.
Word Family: **chivalrous**, *adjective*; **chivalrously**, *adverb*; **chivalrousness**, *noun*.
[Old French *chevalerie*, from *cheval* horse]

This is typical of a *standard* dictionary, but there are other types of dictionaries and wordfinders.

SPELLER'S DICTIONARY

. . . contains list of words in alphabetical order. It doesn't give meanings and other information. This means that it can contain thousands of words but still be light and easy to carry around.

SPELLING BY SOUNDS DICTIONARY

. . . contains words listed the way they sound. For example if you looked up 'foto' it would be in red, with the correct spelling 'photo' after it in black. If you tend to spell the way words sound, it could help. It isn't useful for everyone.

ROGET'S THESAURUS

. . . is similar to a wordfinder but it is not in alphabetical order. It is organised in areas of words about emotion, communication, relationships, etc.

Once you are used to using the index at the back it is easy to find far more interesting words and phrases than you'd get from a wordfinder.

WORDFINDER A–Z

. . . doesn't give meanings but lots of other words which are similar to the one you are looking up.

The words are listed alphabetically and are easy to find. Some wordfinders give you opposites too.

NOTE

Anyone who wants to improve their spelling or their wordpower should make sure that they have a dictionary that is right for them.

Choosing dictionaries

You can buy most dictionaries in pocket size, paperback or large glossy hardback. If you are thinking of buying a dictionary, go to your local bookshop and browse through them. You may be surprised to see how many different types there are. Take your time and see what appeals to you.

Think about:

- whether you want it to carry around with you or to use at home
- whether you need it for spelling, meanings or looking for other words (you may need more than one dictionary)
- the size of print
- the pronunciation guide
- the price – not all expensive ones are the best
- the total vocabulary of words (some dictionaries are short and easy to use but may not contain the words you want)
- the quality of the definition/explanations for words

Using your dictionary to widen your vocabulary:

Find 3 words, from a book or newspaper, which you don't often use in your writing.

Write them here.

1. ....

2. ....

3. ....

Now look each one up in a dictionary and write down the definition or meaning. If you do this regularly, you will get quicker at looking up words and you may start to use a wider vocabulary in your own writing.

Another word for . . .

A thesaurus or other wordfinder can be a great help in improving writing by widening the choice of words. If you don't own one, use the ones in your local library to see if it's worth buying one.

Use a wordfinder or thesaurus to replace the word 'bad' in the following phrases with another that would be more interesting as well as appropriate.

a **bad** experience	a **bad** book	a **bad** report
a **bad** operation	a **bad** apple	a **bad** child
bad handwriting	a **bad** smell	a **bad** day

When you *edit* or tidy up a rough draft of writing (see p.30), you may want to find a better word than the one you jotted down first.

Wordfinders are handy for this and pocket-sized ones are not expensive.

Think about what you could use dictionaries for:

	✔
checking the meaning of words	
checking the spelling of words	
checking on pronunciation	
finding a similar word	
finding an opposite word	
finding new words to use	
finding out about words	

Ask yourself if you need to buy a dictionary or perhaps buy *another* one.

Pocket dictionaries/wordfinders are quite cheap.

Books

There are a few dictionaries among the many available, which deal with certain aspects of spelling and writing. The following list contains some dictionaries which you might find useful.

Wordmaster Dictionary (Penguin, 1987) — Excellent for interesting information about origins of words and phrases.

Heinemann English Dictionary (Heinemann, 1979) — One of the best for an easy guide to pronunciation, e.g. rendezvous, 'ron/day/voo'.

Black's Writing Dictionary (Black, 1972) — Good for lists of words in their different forms (happy/happier/happiness, etc). Clear, easy definitions.

New Collins Thesaurus (Collins, 1984) — A clear, alphabetical wordfinder – (available in pocket size).

Roget's Thesaurus (Penguin, 1984) — Not alphabetical but full of alternative words and phrases.

Pergamon Dictionary of Perfect Spelling (Wheaton, 1979) — Alphabetical lists of words spelt as they sound: e.g. 'foto' – photo.

Aurally Coded English Spelling Dictionary (Learning Development Aids, 1986) — Allows you to find words quickly, providing you know the first letter and the first vowel sound. Good for finding long words.

Things that matter in writing

When you write, how can you make sure your message gets across clearly, accurately and . . . fast? This section offers things to think about when you are producing a piece of written work.

Working at writing

Writing and how much effort you put into it depends on who and what it's for. In order to produce writing that communicates well you need to think about things such as:

> **Preparing . . . Planning . . . Drafting . . . Editing . . . Proofreading**

In amongst these things are several other practical aspects of writing that will also need some thought. They include:

- Grammar
- Punctuation
- Paragraphs
- Spelling
- Handwriting

Grammar

Grammar is about the *rules* of language.

Grammar is part of both *written* and *spoken* language.

Grammar is a way of *structuring meaning*.

Grammar has a vocabulary of its own. Do you recognise some of these?

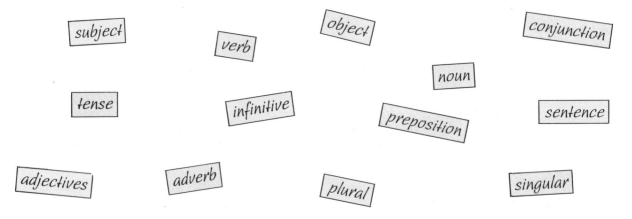

subject   verb   object   conjunction   noun   tense   infinitive   preposition   sentence   adjectives   adverb   plural   singular

Most of us make use of these to good effect without giving them a name. When we read something back to ourselves we can't always explain why one way of writing something seems 'correct', whilst another does not. This is partly because we grow up with language and absorb a lot of its grammar without noticing or ever explaining it to ourselves. These 'instincts' can be useful guides in writing well.

> Used well, grammar will make your writing **flow**.
>
> Used well, grammar will make your **meaning** clear.

Does anything sound wrong to you in these passages of writing?
Make changes if you want to improve grammar, tone or style.

Dear Sir,

<u>Regarding your letter of June 26th, 1989</u>

Please could you telephone me at your convenience to discuss the inflated gas bill you received.

Yours faithfully,

T. Townsend.

Mr. Smith
£196.29
Eastern Gas Co

We was late for the match. We missed the early bus and her leg was plastered so we couldn't walk. The next bus were dead crowded, but on it we got. She couldn't sit down with her leg.

If the baby fails to thrive on untreated milk, boil it.

Dear Miss Honeydew,

I am writing with a happy heart to express my gratitude to you for accompanying me to the Staff Dinner yesterday evening.

Your presence at that experience brought a new dimension to the occasion. I am immensely indebted to you. Perhaps it would be propitious to formalise arrangements for future recreational outings we might wish to consider.

At your convenience, please telephone me so that appropriate discussion can ensue.

Yours sincerely,

Attitudes

Good communication doesn't mean being rigid about using 'correct' grammar. There are many ways of saying the same thing, **but** some people are very pernickety about correct grammar.

If you know you are writing to someone who might be irritated by 'bad' grammar, then you will need to put more energy into composing what you want to say and checking what you have written for mistakes.

- When you write:

  Don't be too fussy and official!
  Don't tie yourself and your reader in knots.
  Don't write long, complicated sentences.

  Do speak and write using language that can easily be understood and which won't come over as nonsense.

- *As a rule of thumb:* If something *sounds* right to you when you read it back to yourself it will probably *sound* right to the reader too. If you are not sure ask someone for their opinion. If you feel you want or need to look at grammar in more depth try some books on the subject.

Basic English Exercises, E.H. Edwards (Macmillan, 1979).

16+ English, M. Baber (Stanley Thornes, 1982).

Punctuation

For most of us punctuation is wrapped up in words like these:

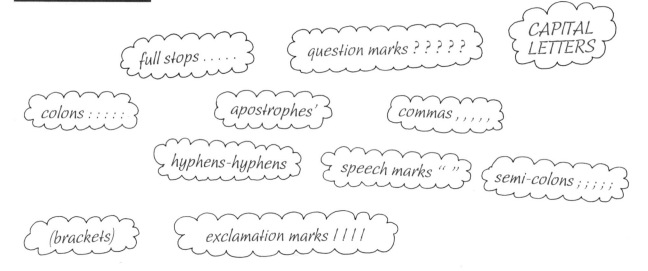

Some sound peculiar. Some sound vaguely medical! They may remind you of boring exercises at school.

In fact . . .

We can all punctuate even if we can't spell! We do it every time we speak. We time our words, put in pauses to break up what we are saying into units of meaning, and change our tone of voice or speaking speed to get different effects.

Listen to yourself on tape if you want to hear punctuation in action.

For readers

- Punctuation helps a reader make sense and understand the emphasis and order in a written message.

- Punctuation helps a reader hear the writer's voice.

Try reading something aloud from the newspaper. Notice how much you need the punctuation to help you read it sensibly.

For writers

- Writers use punctuation to take control of the page.
- Writers use punctuation to help them put over their meaning.
- Punctuation helps the writer to make his voice heard in the way he wants it to be heard.

Words on their own are not enough!

Look through the following example starting with the completely unmarked text:

```
theclarionsrightofreplycolumnmillionairebuys
thethamesamillionairehasboughttheriver
thamestheonlytroubleishisassetskeepfloating
awaysoheintendstospendanothertwomillionpounds
boxingtheriverinateachendthishasbeenstrongly
opposedbythelondonwaterauthorityaspokesman
fortheauthoritysaidweareverymuchagainstthisas
theriverwouldthenbecomeareservoirthematteristo
bedebatedinparliamentwhatareyourviewswrite
inandletusknow
```

We can sort it out bit by bit by:

1. Putting spaces between the words.

```
the  clarions right of reply column
millionaire buys the thames a millionaire has
bought the river thames the only trouble is
his assets keep floating away so he intends to
spend another two million pounds boxing the
river in at each end this has been strongly
opposed by the london water authority a
spokesman for the authority said we are very
much against this as the river would then
become a reservoir the matter is to be
debated in parliament what are your views
write in and let us know
```

2. Using some punctuation marks – full stops, commas, etc.

```
the  clarion's right of reply column.
millionaire buys the thames! a millionaire has
bought the river thames. the only trouble is
his assets keep floating away, so he intends to
spend another two million pounds boxing the
river in at each end. this has been strongly
opposed by the london water authority. a
spokesman for the authority said, "we are very
much against this as the river would then
become a reservoir." the matter is to be
debated in parliament. what are your views?
write in and let us know.
```

3. Using capital letters (also known as 'upper-case' letters).

```
The Clarion's Right of Reply Column.
Millionaire buys the Thames! A millionaire has
bought the River Thames. The only trouble is
his assets keep floating away, so he intends to
spend another two million pounds boxing the
river in at each end. This has been strongly
opposed by the London Water Authority. A
spokesman for the Authority said, "We are very
much against this as the river would then
become a reservoir." The matter is to be
debated in Parliament. What are your views?
Write in and let us know.
```

4. Involving paragraphs, spacing and headings.

```
The Clarion's Right of Reply Column.

MILLIONAIRE BUYS THE THAMES!

A millionaire has bought the River Thames. The
only trouble is his assets keep floating away,
so he intends to spend another two million
pounds boxing the river in at each end. This
has been strongly opposed by the London Water
Authority. A spokesman for the Authority said,

"We are very much against this as the river
would then become a reservoir."

The matter is to be debated in Parliament.
What are your views? Write in and let us know.
```

The finished piece might actually look something like this:

THE CLARION'S RIGHT OF REPLY COLUMN

MILLIONAIRE BUYS THE THAMES!

A MILLIONAIRE has bought the River Thames. The only trouble is his assets keep floating away, so he intends to spend another two million pounds boxing the river in at each end. This has been strongly opposed by the London Water Authority. A spokesman for the Authority said,

"We are very much against this as the river would then become a reservoir."

The matter is to be debated in Parliament.

What are YOUR views? Write in and let us know.

The final version of the text in the last activity used various punctuation marks.

Punctuation marks

Full Stops

A full stop means STOP. It means you have made a complete statement. It marks the end of a sentence. It is followed by a capital letter:

e.g. *He set off up the mountain.*
His pace was brisk and strong.

Speech Marks

Are used to show the words actually being spoken by someone. Sometimes they are called 'inverted commas':

e.g. *"I want to come" said Peter, "but I just don't have enough cash."*

Exclamation Marks

Are used to show alarm. Or surprise. Or to give emphasis and drama to a word or statement:

e.g. *Fire!*
It was fabulous!
I don't believe it!

Question Marks

These show that a question has been asked:

e.g. *What time is it?*
Why are you crying?
Is that it?

Paragraphs

Usually more than one sentence about the same theme, idea or topic, grouped together on a page.

Commas

Make you pause. They are used for:

- Lists:
  e.g. *I picked up paper, a pencil, a ruler and a box of crayons.*

- Putting extra bits into a sentence:
  e.g. *In the morning, all being well, I am off to Scotland.*

- Breaking up long sentences:
  e.g. *The three men sitting on the docks, which were otherwise deserted, stared out nervously over the water.*

 **ACTIVITY**

Look back at the final draft of the 'Clarion's Right of Reply Column' and see how these punctuation marks were actually used.

Capital letters were also used a great deal in that example.

These are not seen as punctuation marks by everyone, but they certainly play a vital role in marking out meaning in the text and making it easy to read.

Capital letters begin sentences and proper names, such as towns, countries, months and days. They are also often used for the main words in titles:

A Tale of Two Cities

Land of Hope and Glory

Indiana Jones and . . .

Policy Document: Services for People with Impaired Hearing

More punctuation

There are at least 5 other punctuation marks which, as a reader or a writer, you should be aware of.

Semi-colons

These are rather like commas, but make you pause longer. The two parts of a sentence joined with a semi-colon are too closely related to be separated by a full stop.

e.g. *The dog was starving; its ribs were sticking out of its skin.*

Dashes

These can be used to add afterthoughts,

e.g. *I'd lost all my money – £20 at least.*

They can also be used instead of commas,

e.g. *If you go – whatever the time – let me know.*

Brackets (or parentheses)

These are sometimes used instead of commas. They allow the writer to put extra information into a sentence which will add to its overall meaning,

e.g. *The repair man will call (probably later on this afternoon) to sort out the photocopier.*

Note: If you take a set of brackets and the words inside them out of a sentence, it will still make sense.

Colons

These are used between two long, but closely connected, or contrasting sentences,

e.g. *One child was lost in a story book: the other was crying and staring out of the window.*

They can also go before a list, especially in business letters,

e.g. *This note should go to several departments: Accounts, Graphics, Sales, Servicing.*

Apostrophes

These are used to show that letters have been left out,

e.g. *wasn't (was not)*
you've (you have)

Or, to show who or what owns something,

e.g. *the dog's bone*
Tom's car
the manager's decision

Note: If there is more than one owner or the owner's name ends in an s, then the apostrophe goes after the s,
e.g. *James' house*
the hens' eggs
the four boys' bicycles

A. Look at the effect punctuation can have on sense and meaning. See if you can punctuate this line of writing in two different ways to change the meaning and emphasis.

> will you be ready for your sisters party at 7 love eve.

B. Punctuate this passage and then re-write it using the layout that you think suits it best. Check your work against the original below.

```
the ordeal of james bartley
the most amazing story you will find in the whole literature of
travel is that a man has been actually swallowed by a whale and
lived to tell the tale in 1891 the american whaler star of the
east was off the falkland islands when in the excitement and
confusion of a catch a seaman named james bartley went overboard
and was given up for lost the whale was killed brought alongside
and stripped of its blubber next day the stomach was searched for
the valuable ambergris which is often found in unpleasant
surroundings of this nature the men noticed that something alive
seemed to be stirring in the folds and creases and when they
investigated they found the doubled up and unconscious figure
of bartley he was delirious for a fortnight but when he recovered
sufficiently to tell his story he said that when he went
overboard he seemed to enter a warm moving passage presently he
found himself in the whales stomach where the heat was terrific
but where a certain amount of air reached him bartley recovered
completely from his terrible ordeal except for the fact that
his skin became a fixed bleached white
```

Possible answers to A

Will you be ready for your sisters? Party at 7. Love, Eve.

Will you be ready for your sister's party at 7? Love, Eve.

Will. You be ready for your sister's party at 7! Love, Eve.

Will you be ready for your sister's party at 7, love? Eve.

The ordeal of James Bartley

The most amazing story you will find in the whole literature of travel is that a man has been actually swallowed by a whale and lived to tell the tale. In 1891 the American whaler *Star of the East* was off the Falkland Islands when, in the excitement and confusion of a catch, a seaman named James Bartley went overboard and was given up for lost. The whale was killed, brought alongside and stripped of its blubber. Next day the stomach was searched for the valuable ambergris which is often found in unpleasant surroundings of this nature. The men noticed that something alive seemed to be stirring in the folds and creases, and when they investigated they found the doubled-up and unconscious figure of Bartley.

He was delirious for a fortnight, but when he recovered sufficiently to tell his story he said that when he went over-board he seemed to enter a warm moving passage. Presently he found himself in the whale's stomach, where the heat was terrific but where a certain amount of air reached him.

Bartley recovered completely from his terrible ordeal, except for the fact that his skin became a fixed bleached white.

- Punctuation helps writers make sense for readers.
- Use punctuation purposefully.

Look through a newspaper article. Use a highlighter pen to mark all the punctuation used. Decide why it has been used. If you don't know, ask someone, or see if any of this section or the following suggested books can help.

Spelling and Punctuation, Denys Thompson (OUP, 1984).

Mind the Stop, G.V. Carey (Penguin, 1989).

Paragraphs

Paragraphs are sometimes regarded as part of punctuation, but, like sentences, they are really about organising text into meaningful 'bite-sized' chunks.

> **Sentence:** a fairly short statement that makes complete sense on its own.
>
> **Paragraph:** sometimes one sentence, but usually several sentences related to the same point, theme or topic, grouped together on the page.

Paragraphs:

- organise meaning on the page.
- help to hold the meaning and flow of the writing together.
- break up text so that it isn't too dense and off-putting to the reader.
- always begin on a new line, either a little way in from the margin or at the margin edge itself, perhaps with a line of space above.

Some of the other important effects of layout have been shown in the punctuation example on p.17.

Spelling

Not all 'good' writers are 'good' spellers, because there's a lot more to writing than spelling well.

A piece of writing could be full of spelling errors but be more interesting than a perfectly spelled passage, because of what it has to say and the way it says it.

Perspectives and attitudes

- It is important to keep spelling in perspective.
- We need to think about when it matters most.
- It need not be 100% correct for everything we write.

In these first 2 examples spelling is not that important:

Dear Gran,
My freind Jane and I
wood like to come for the
weekend . I know . . . . .

6 eggs
1 Cabbidge
5lbs potatos
2lb apples
6 orranges

Spelling does matter a lot if:

it causes the reader to 'judge' the writer as stupid or ill-educated or uncaring about how he/she writes.

it annoys the reader, so that he/she loses interest in the writing and perhaps then underestimates both the writing and the writer.

it is so bad that it stops the reader from getting at what the writing is trying to say.

ACTIVITY

How do you feel about your own spelling skills? Where do you think you are in terms of developing them? Read the two lists below and tick the phrases that best describe *you* and *your* spelling at the moment.

A.

I don't mind writing but I feel bad about the spelling errors. ☐

I often know when I've got a word wrong. ☐

I can usually tell which bit of the word is wrong. ☐

It's funny how I often get long words right but make mistakes with easy words. ☐

B.

I hate writing because I think I can't spell – I try not to write at all. ☐

I can't tell if I've spelt a word wrong. ☐

How can I check my spelling if I don't know which ones are right or wrong? ☐

If you've ticked more boxes in the 'A' list then you are well on your way to improving your spelling by analysing your errors and strengths.

If you've ticked more boxes in the 'B' list you need to ask someone who you know is a good speller to help you identify your errors and strengths so that you can start improving your spelling.

Useful spelling information and techniques

Wherever you are with your spelling these two pages will show you some ways of tackling the most common problems.

---

1. The English **alphabet** only has 26 letters but they have to be used to make at least 44 different sounds. Don't rely too heavily on the sounds in a word to help you spell it. Better to **look** at the patterns of letters in words. They might not sound the same, but they may use the same group of letters and look similar.

Think about:

rough   **though**   **ought**   **cough**   **bough**   **through**

---

2. Use spelling pronunciation to help you fix a word in your mind. For some words this means you **say** all the bits of it when you are remembering its spelling, even though that's not how it is normally said.

e.g. We say Wensday . . . We spell it **Wed-nes-day**
We say Febry . . . We spell it **Feb-ru-ary**

---

3. Use rules if they help.

e.g. In the plural change y into i and add es – family/**families,**
lorry/**lorries.**

---

4. **Build** on what you know already.

e.g. You can spell **board,** so . . . that's half of

sideboard   chipboard   cardboard   blackboard   hard......

You can spell **garden,** so . . . that's most of

garden<u>er</u>   garden<u>s</u>   garden<u>ed</u>   garden<u>ing</u>

---

5. Use **mnemonics** if they help. These are tricks or hooks to help you recall awkward spellings.

e.g. An island . . . **is land**

Embar**r**ass . . . That's two r's because you're **really red!**

---

6. **Visualise.** Try to picture words so that their meaning and spelling make an image in your head.

e.g.

7. Know that some words **sound** the same but are **spelled** differently and **mean** different things.

e.g. **rode** and **road** and **rowed**

or

reign and **rein** and **rain**

Spotting spelling mistakes

It is perhaps more important to be able to spot your spelling errors during proofreading than it is to be an amazingly perfect speller . . . of only a few words!

Good writers develop a feel for words. They start to know when they **look right** and when they **look wrong.** This skill means that they can just get on with writing what they want to say to begin with and then they can check through later, before they do a fair copy.

Look through a piece of your own first draft writing. How many errors can you spot? Can you correct any of them straight away? What are you going to do about the others?

You could:

| Use a dictionary | or | Ask someone | or | Have another shot at it |

Can you spot the 13 spelling mistakes in this piece of writing? First of all, circle possibilities in pencil. Then check them.

> For my work experiane I went to a local libary. It was a bransh libary. When I arived I introduced myself to the assistent libarian. She showed me round the vareous sections and explaned the different prosedures. On my first day I went out with the house-bound servis for the ellderly. We visited about eigteen old people. It was all very interesting and I enjayed talking to them.

If you think of yourself as a bad speller and it worries you, then perhaps you should do something about it. You *will* have to work at it, but it *will* be worth it if it makes you feel better about writing. And bear in mind these points.

- Always proofread your written work.
- Ask someone else to check it as well if you want to.
- Make good use of a dictionary.
- Try to learn a few new words each week and revise them regularly.
- Keep words you often use, but have difficulty in spelling, on a personal list.

ASSIGNMENTS Try to write for at least ten minutes twice a week. Use what you write to look at the kinds of spelling mistakes you are making, and try to work out why. If you can, discuss things with someone else.

Remember that words are all around you. Try to start looking at them more carefully so that you begin to notice things about the way they are spelled.

Books

Spelling Matters, Bernard Sadler (E. Arnold, 1982).

Spelling It Out, Rhiannedd Pratley (BBC Books, 1988).

Spelling Pack (ALBSU, 1988).

Handwriting

This section is about putting pen to paper and the effect that handwriting can have on readers and writing!

Clear, readable handwriting is an asset! You can't really quibble with that.

> **Fair or not** – Research shows that in exams teachers and examiners tend to give higher marks when the handwriting is good.
>
> **Fair or not** – When employers are considering hundreds of applications for a handful of jobs, you can hardly blame them for homing in on those that are easy to read!

Above all else, handwriting is an important aspect of communication:

- If it's *illegible,* there's not much point in writing.
- If it's *badly formed,* or very *unusual* it will slow the reader down. When this happens the reader may lose interest or underestimate what's written.
- Someone faced with bad handwriting may make *unfair judgements* about the writer's character, ability or education.

BUT

- Handwriting should not be seen as a set of rigid rules.
- It should display character and individuality.
- It should vary from person to person.

Feelings about handwriting

Some people have really lovely handwriting. They enjoy putting pen to paper. They like the look of their work when it's finished. Other people hate their handwriting.

How do you feel about your handwriting?

I don't like it		*It's not bad*		*I like it*	

See if other people agree with you.

Clarity in handwriting

More than anything clear handwriting will help the writer to communicate effectively. Clarity can be badly affected by a whole host of often quite minor points such as:

- Writing style, e.g. too fussy, too small, too cramped, too large.
- How much time the writer had to do the writing!
- What the writer was writing on . . . and with.
- Whether the writer had a steady hand.
- Whether the writer was being watched as he wrote.
- The writer's poor eyesight.
- Carelessly formed letters.
- Lack of confidence about writing at all.

Look at a piece of your own writing. Think about when, where and why you wrote it. Do any of the points on the above list apply?

Now take time to look closely at the letters themselves:

- Do you form your letters carefully?
- Are your letters fairly consistent in their size?
- Do the sticks on letters like h and b or p and g get tangled up with the letters on the line above or below?
- Do you write in a mixture of CAPITALS and small letters like this

  unNecEssARy

- Do you use capitals at the start of words whenever the mood takes you rather than when they are called for?
- Does your writing lean *this way and that*?
- Do you join letters up in an awkward way?

Decide what you *do like* about your writing. Decide what you *don't like* about it.

Make two lists.

Are you happy to leave it at that?

Making changes

If you don't feel your handwriting is good enough for your needs, think about improving it. You don't have to change your style completely: you might prefer just to tidy it up a bit.

If you are going to make changes you will have to think about how you will alter the things you don't like. You will also need to practise your new writing to make it your own and so that you can do it without thinking.

Handwriting and spelling

One way we remember things is through our memory of movement. Writing can help spelling in this way. In fact, good spellers find their pen almost seems to write the words their brain is thinking of on its own!

> **Fluent handwriting can actually help with spelling.**

The more flowing your handwriting style the better, because it means that words won't get 'interrupted'. Spellings will become complete little patterns of movement.

You don't have to be a beautiful writer, just think about how you write now and how it might be improved so that you write more quickly, smoothly and clearly.

 **ACTIVITY**   Bearing these points in mind, which of these styles do you think would be most helpful to spelling?

> *beautiful*   *beautiful*   *beautiful*
>
> BEAUTIFUL   *beautiful*   beautiful   BeAuTiFuL

- Remember that your writing is part of you.
- It doesn't always have to be done carefully. That depends on the situation and the time you have, so be practical about it.

Mum
Back at 1

Dear Mr. James,
I am writing to....

- Write with a pen you like. The right tools for the job make a big difference.

ASSIGNMENTS   Look at other people's writing. Pinch the bits you like!

Copy things out sometimes so that you are practising writing and not thinking about what to write.

Maybe you could find out about Calligraphy

It's really an art form rather than handwriting, but it's lovely to look at, fun to learn . . . and it impresses friends no end!

 Books   *How to Improve Your Handwriting*, Martin Good (NEC, 1983).

Teach Yourself Handwriting, Sassoon & Briem (Hodder & Stoughton, 1984).

Getting started with writing

This section looks at collecting ideas or information in order to get started with a piece of writing. This process leads to your *first draft* or *rough copy*.

Why write?

We write because we need to } for work, home, study, to give instructions,
or because we want to } opinions, keep in touch ... etc.

Some people avoid writing for different reasons. You may agree with some of these:

	✓
I'm not sure of what to say.	
People will see how bad I am at spelling, handwriting, punctuation, etc.	
I know what to say but I'm not sure how to put it down.	
It never looks or sounds right when I've written it.	
I'm no good at writing – they told me that at school.	
I'll telephone instead.	
I always make mistakes and keep having to start again.	
The blank sheet of paper puts me off.	

The hardest part for many people is getting started. Even if they know what they want to say, they are worried about putting pen to paper. This is often because they think that *all* writing should be:

✓ neat   ✓ in proper sentences

✓ well set out ✓ free of mistakes

This may be true in some cases, but not for *all* writing and certainly not when you are just jotting down ideas or doing a *rough copy*.

Rough copies or first drafts	don't need to be	☒ neat
		☒ well set out
		☒ in proper sentences
		☒ free of mistakes

Only the *final* copy matters and the first thing we write is not normally the perfect, final copy.

What makes a good writer?

It isn't easy to say why some people are better writers than others. But there are some things that are worth knowing:

Good writers

- have some *confidence* in their own ideas and ability.
- realise that good writing doesn't always happen; it needs *developing*.
- think about the *purpose* of their writing (and *who* will read it).
- don't worry too much about messiness or mistakes in rough copies.
- *work* at a piece until they are happy with it (see Editing on p.30).
- are not always good at spelling, punctuation and grammar.

Tips for getting started

Tick one or two points which you could try to help you to get started.

	✓
Use a pencil – it may help you to think of it as a rough copy	
Double space – in other words leave a line of space between your lines of writing to make room for changes	
Try to write when you are in the mood for writing	
If you can't think, take a short break from your work, and then return to it	
Think of your rough draft as something to be worked on	
Don't throw it away at the first mistake – carry on	
Don't use your best paper – save that for the final copy	
Try different ways of getting started and find out which ones work for you	

There are many ways of getting started and they are all good, providing they suit **you** and your **purpose** in writing.

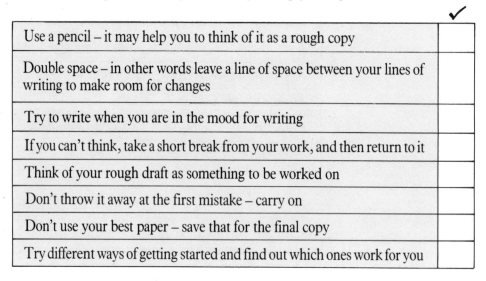

The following examples show 3 of these methods:

- Brainstorming
- Writing as it comes
- Using a wordprocessor

Brainstorming

Brainstorming is when you let *all* your ideas come out in a rush or a storm. You don't stop to think about them. That comes later. You get down as many ideas as you can quickly (see **A**). Then you select some (or all of them!) and write something about each (see **B**).

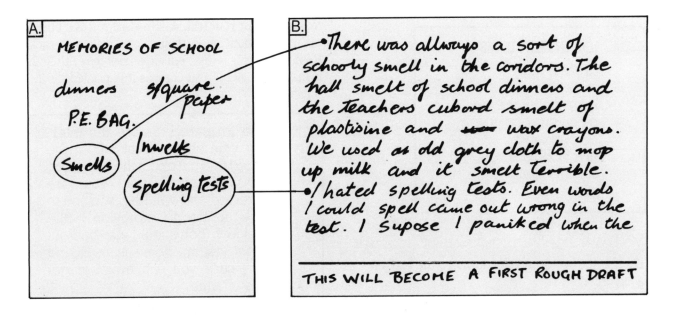

Writing as it comes

Writing as it comes is good if you can write quickly (it doesn't matter about spelling or neatness at this stage). Just scribble down whatever comes to mind (see **A**). (It's like thinking on paper.) Then read through what you have written and pick out the main points. Take these points and write a bit more (or less) about each (see **B**).

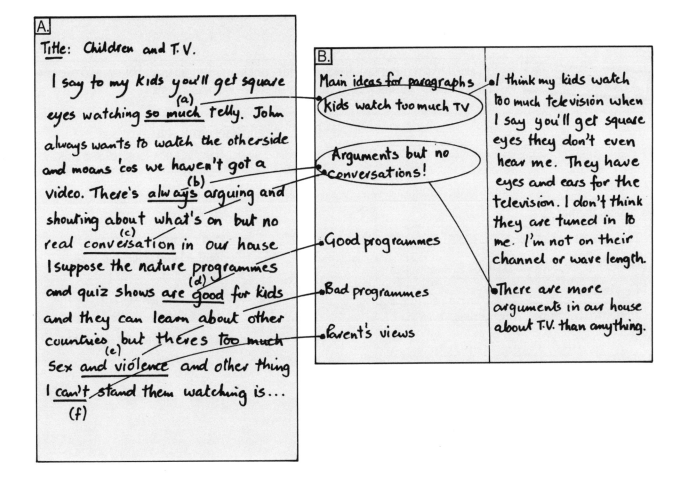

Using a wordprocessor

Using a wordprocessor can help with several ways of starting. It is good for adding bits, rearranging or just collecting ideas. You never need to re-write, you just *change* what you have typed in.

A. Type in the headings or ideas as they come to you.

> **A**
>
> **JOB INTERVIEWS**
> dress right
> smile, etc
> know about the job
> be on time
> be prepared
> give good answers
> ask questions
> sit properly

B. Use the wordprocessor to move the text into a good order.

> **B**
> 1. Be prepared
> 2. Dress right
> 3. Be on time
> 4. Body language
> 5. Answer questions well
> 6. Ask questions

C. Now you have an order, you can put in lines to make space for your text. At this stage you don't need to worry about any typing or spelling errors. Remember, this is just your first *rough copy* although it may seem like a neat copy as it is printed on the screen.

> **C**
> 1. Be Prepared. Before the interview yoiu should think about the job and find out about the company. This will show that you are interested and will help you you to make a good impresion atthe intreview. You should also find out where the interview is held and make sure you can travel to get there on time.
>
> 2. Dress Right When you go for your interview you should be dressed suitably for the job. For example, you wouldn't wear a . . . . . .
> 3. Be on Time
> 4. Body Language
> 5. Answer Questions Well
> 6. Ask Questions

ASSIGNMENT

1. Take a real writing task from your life, or choose a topic from below, and use one of the methods in this section (or your own) to do a *rough copy*.

Litter and pollution	
Retirement at 50?	
School memories	
Reasons for retraining as a . . .	
Giving up smoking (or trying to)	
Football violence	
Letter to the council complaining about	
or your choice	

BUT

Before you start

- have a quick look back at this section.

- remind yourself that it's only a rough copy.

- don't worry if you try a new method and it feels strange at first.

- if you can't get started, use the sample boxes on the next page.

- REMEMBER: the main thing is *get started*.

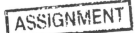

Brainstorming

1. Write your chosen title here ....

2. Now think, as quickly as you can, of all possible ideas about your chosen title.

3. Write each one in a box – just a word or two.

4. Now look at each box and write a few sentences about the idea you put down (you don't need to do them all – choose a few).

5. Decide on a good order for the ideas and have a go at writing a first *rough draft*.

If you do the assignments in the other sections or have a writing task to do at home or at work, **remember:**

*   rough drafts are an important part of writing

*   rough drafts are meant to be messy and have errors

*   there are lots of ways to get started

Make a note for yourself of the things from this section that you intend to *use* or *think about* for your future rough drafts.

....

....

....

....

....

....

Editing and proofreading

Once you have put pen to paper and have done a rough draft (see Getting Started with Writing on p.25) you are ready to work on it.

This section looks at developing your

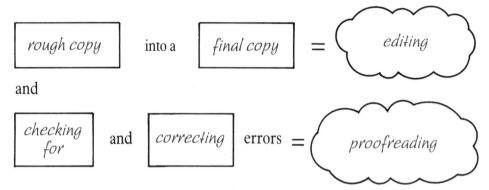

and

What do you think about editing and proofreading?		✓
I've never done it. I can't be bothered	A	
I don't know how to improve my rough copy	B	
I'm just happy to get anything down – it will have to do	C	
'Editing' and 'proofreading' sound too technical	D	
It sounds like a long job to me	E	
I already proofread and edit my written work	F	

If you ticked any of the points, you may like to read our comments:

A	If you are interested in developing your writing skills, you may *need* to bother!
B	This section will show you some ways of improving your rough drafts.
C	Sometimes your first rough copy *will* do, however scrappy it looks. The real skill is knowing *when* it needs to be worked on and that's where this section will help you.
D	The words sound grand but they are just another way of saying 'getting it right'.
E	Yes, it can take time at first, but if it is an important piece of writing then it should be worth the effort. Once you have mastered the skills of *editing* and *proofreading*, you'll find that, with practice, you can do it quite quickly.
F	If you already feel confident about editing and proofreading, you may not need to work on this section. However, you could glance through, just to see if anything catches your eye.

Editing

When good writers (at any level) edit their writing, they think about several things:

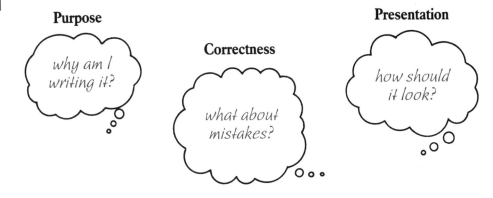

Audience
who will be reading it?

Purpose
why am I writing it?

Correctness
what about mistakes?

Presentation
how should it look?

Thinking about these things will help to decide *whether* to edit or not, *how* to edit and *what* the final copy should be like.

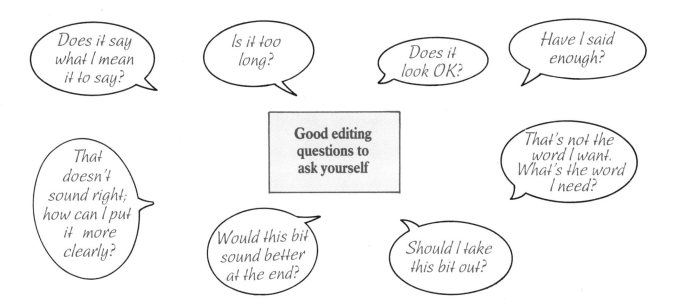

Does it say what I mean it to say?

Is it too long?

Does it look OK?

Have I said enough?

Good editing questions to ask yourself

That doesn't sound right; how can I put it more clearly?

That's not the word I want. What's the word I need?

Would this bit sound better at the end?

Should I take this bit out?

Proofreading

When writers proofread, they are looking for mistakes in *spelling*, *punctuation* and *grammar*. (These 3 areas are covered in more detail on p.10.)

Sometimes the mistakes are just 'slips of the pen' (or typing errors) because we usually do rough drafts quickly. The most common errors to look for are:
spelling and **words missed out.**

- Try to read through your writing as if you've never seen it before (otherwise you tend to read what you *think* is there).

- Think about the sort of mistakes you often make (e.g. forgetting to drop the 'e' when you add 'ing') and look out for them.

- If it's an important letter or other formal writing, get someone else to proofread it as well.

REMEMBER

If you proofread your own work it is easy to read what you *think* is there rather than what you've *actually* written.

Examples of editing and proofreading

Not everything you write needs to be edited or proofread. Leaving a note for family or a friend can be scribbled and misspelt but as long as he or she can read it that's all that really matters.

Here are some examples of writing which *do* need to be edited and proofread:

This letter looks neat because it has been wordprocessed on a computer. However ▼ it needs editing and proofreading to look like this. ▼

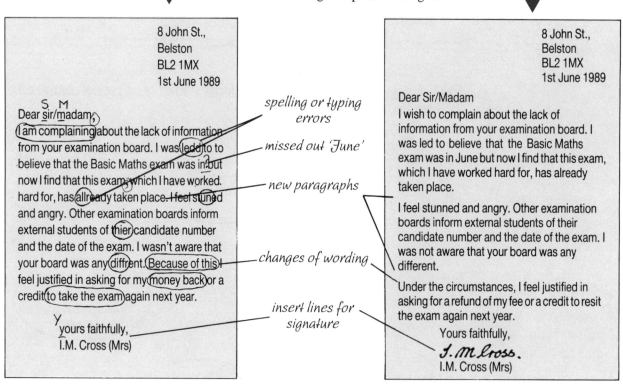

If you can use a wordprocessor you won't need to re-write everything. You can just overtype, put in spaces, change words or move bits around

In the same way, handwritten pieces need editing and proofreading. This may mean re-writing but sometimes it's worth the effort.

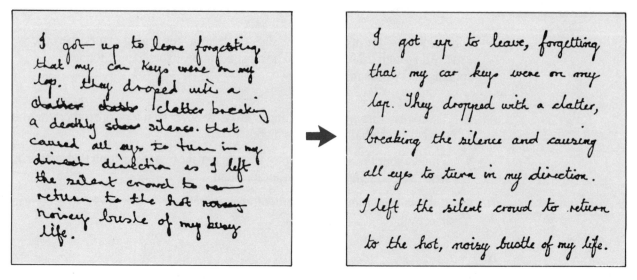

In the re-written version, the writer has changed spelling, phrases, punctuation *and* improved the handwriting. This has made the piece easier to read.

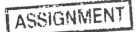

You'll need a rough draft of a piece of writing for this assignment. (Getting Started with Writing on p.25 will help you do a rough draft.)

First *edit* your rough draft, using the information from this section.

Then *proofread* it for errors.

You may find the checklist at the bottom of this page helps to remind you of the areas to think about. You should also read pp.10-24, which deal with how grammar, punctuation, presentation and spelling can affect a piece of writing.

Whenever you *edit a rough draft* to turn it into your *final copy*, think of the points covered in this section. Think especially about:

- PURPOSE
- AUDIENCE
- PRESENTATION
- CORRECTNESS

You may find this checklist helpful (or you could make your own).

Checklist for editing to final copy		✔
AUDIENCE	Is it right for my reader?	
	Will they understand it?	
	Have I used the best words/tone?	
PURPOSE	Have I said what I wanted to say?	
	Is it clear? Does it sound OK?	
	Is it the best order for the purpose?	
PRESENTATION	Does it look OK? (neatness, etc.)	
	Is the paper and pen colour/type OK?	
	Is it properly spaced and paragraphed?	
CORRECTNESS	Is the spelling, punctuation, etc. OK?	
	Have I checked that the information is correct?	

Letters and letter writing

Dear Reader,
This section is about writing letters. Do you write letters? How often? What kinds? Who to? Do you like writing letters? Do you like receiving letters? If you are a letter writer or want to be a letter writer this section could be of interest to you.

Why write letters?

Despite the telephone, letters remain a very important form of communication.

| They can be read again. | They can be put together carefully. |
| They may be the only option. | They are a permanent record. |

Letters are an effective way of passing on information, of expressing views, of making things happen, of staying in touch.

How many of these letters have you ever had to write?

| ✓ | ✗ | ? |

	✓✗?		✓✗?
To ask for information		To someone in hospital	
To give information		To excuse a child's absence	
To family and friends		To ask a favour	
To express sympathy		To air a view	
To apologise		To offer congratulations	
To say thanks		To a newspaper or magazine	
To offer or accept an invitation		To a fan club	
To order or return goods		To confirm a phone call	
To accept or turn down a job		To ask permission	
To resign		To press for action	
To complain		For work	
To go with an application form for a job or a course		To an agony column for help or advice	

Letters can vary greatly in style and it's important to know about the best ways of writing different kinds of letters. There are lots of shades in between, but letters are usually divided roughly into two groups:

> **Informal Letters:** use English that is friendly and chatty, rather as we speak.
>
> **Formal Letters:** use English that sounds rather more official; they don't sound the way people usually talk.

Writing effective letters

This means:

- Being aware of **who** you are writing to.
- Being sure of the **purpose** of your letter.

It also means:

- *Knowing* about the different styles of language, page layout, paper and writing rules that are right for some letters.
- *Recognising* that handwriting might be a problem sometimes.
- *Accepting* that doing a rough draft first could be a good idea in some instances, especially in order to get spelling, punctuation, your choice of words and the organisation of your ideas right.
- *Using* the right tools for the job – pencil is rarely very acceptable.
- *Learning* to use language that suits the audience and the purpose. Even holiday postcards can be very different depending on who they are sent to . . .

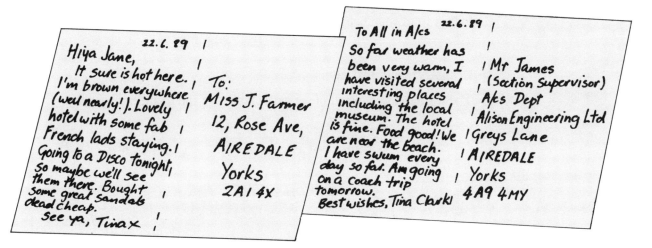

Addresses

These are usually written as shown on the postcards above. Either they are 'indented' as on the first postcard, or 'blocked' as on the second one.

- On envelopes make sure you leave plenty of room for the *stamp* and *post mark*.

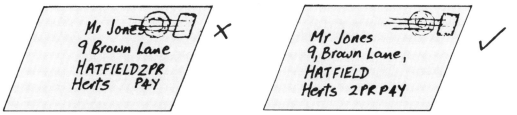

- Put the name of the town in CAPITALS.

  Use the *post code* if you know it. This will speed up sorting and delivery.

- Sometimes you may need to write *extra information* on the outside of the envelope. Do it *clearly* without interfering with the address.

Informal letters

Informal letters are mainly written to family and friends and should be fairly chatty in style.

They should also be:

- *Interesting to* the reader
- *Interested in* the reader
- *Linked* to previous letters

You could include

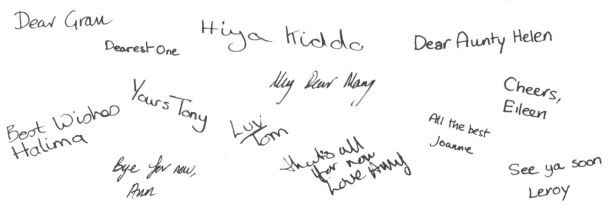

questions · opinions · requests · answers · invitations · news · thanks · apologies · worries · suggestions

You might do a rough draft of an informal letter first, but more than likely you won't bother, because really you are 'talking' to people you know well and who are just glad to hear from you. You might still want to jot down a list of things before you start.

Openings to informal letters

These are almost a matter of personal choice . . . and so are endings .

Dear Gran

Dearest One

Hiya Kiddo

Dear Aunty Helen

My Dear Mary

Best Wishes Halima

Yours Tony

Luv Tom

Cheers, Eileen

Bye for now, Ann

That's all for now Love Amy

All the best Joanne

See ya soon Leroy

Mostly you will simply add your first name after your chosen ending.

Layout for an informal letter

Example 1 is one way of organising a simple letter.
Example 2 is there for you to rearrange in a similar way.

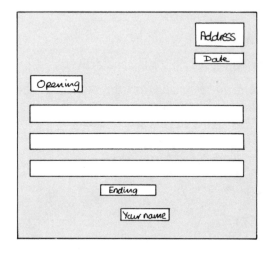

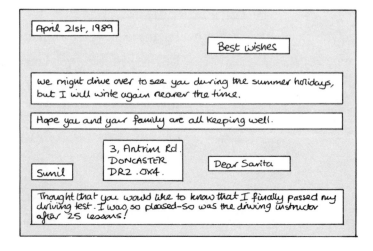

Formal informal letters!

Some letters to people you know quite well might be written in a more formal way because of their purpose.

Dear Uncle Joe,

a. A few lines to make contact again and to explain why you are writing ie. you want a favour

b. more details about what you want and why; who you will be borrowing from etc.

c. What your Uncle will have to do and be responsible for if he agrees to be your guaranter

d. Some kind of reassurance about your role in all of this! You can afford the repayments etc.

e. A final few words about next steps, the time scale and your thanks if the request can be agreed to

Best wishes
Louise

1. You want an uncle to act as guarantor for a loan you hope to take out.

Paragraphs for different purposes to make sure all the facts are clear.

2. You have to write a letter of condolence.

Dear Mr and Mrs Charles,

I was so sorry to hear of Tania's sudden death. It must have come as a terrible shock to you and all the family.

Everyone at work extends their sympathy to you. We shall miss her as she was always so pleasant to be with and helpful to all newcomers.

She will not be forgotten easily....

3. You want to cheer up someone who's sick or in hospital.

DON'T

1. Don't dwell on the illness or its consequences!
2. Don't go on about everything the person's missing out on!
3. Don't include insensitive references to other sick people or tragedies
4. Don't go on about your own troubles

DO

Offer support: write interesting news
Bring people up to date: Suggest things to do: Be lighthearted where you can.
Look to the future if you can.

- You could send a card.
- Best to be straightforward.
- Be sensitive.
- Refer to the dead person's good qualities.
- Don't raise any other subject in this letter.

NOTE

When you write these letters try to imagine how the person will feel and write as if you are talking to them.

Formal letters

lobbying for action

business

legal matters

resignation

complaints

requests on behalf of . . .

job applications

references

These kinds of letters are usually seen as *formal* letters. They should still be interesting, informative and easy to read, but they should also stick to rules and conventions more closely than informal letters.

Why do you think this is? Try to think of three reasons. You will find some answers in the rest of this section.

It is nearly always a good idea to keep a copy of this type of letter for your own records.

Layout for a formal letter

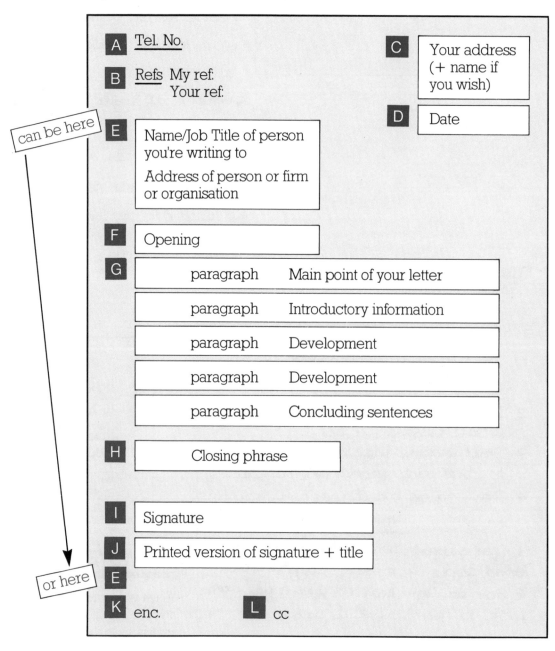

A — Tel. No.

B — Refs My ref:
          Your ref:

C — Your address (+ name if you wish)

D — Date

can be here

E — Name/Job Title of person you're writing to

Address of person or firm or organisation

F — Opening

G — paragraph Main point of your letter

paragraph Introductory information

paragraph Development

paragraph Development

paragraph Concluding sentences

H — Closing phrase

I — Signature

J — Printed version of signature + title

or here E

K enc. L cc

A

Tel. No = telephone number.
You may need to be contacted quickly; a telephone number (work and/or home) could be very helpful sometimes.

B

Refs = references.
You may have a reference number (or letters) for your correspondence. If you have, use it where shown on the example. It will help to connect your letter with past correspondence about the same matter.

The same applies to the 'addressee' (the person you are writing to). If they have used a reference in other letters about this particular matter, then use it for the same reasons.

C

Your home or business address as appropriate.

D

The date you are writing the letter or passing it for typing.

E

The name and job title of the person you are writing to (if known), plus their address. This can be vital if your letter is going to a large organisation. A letter might go round several departments before reaching the right person if it is not immediately clear from the letter who it is for.

F

Openings = ways of starting the letter itself.
The opening has a line all to itself.
Openings are also known as *salutations* and *greetings*.

If you are writing to a particular person, but you don't know their name, use the following openings:

Dear Sir   Dear Madam   Dear Sir/Madam

If you have *no idea* who is likely to deal with your letter, begin:

Dear Sirs

If the letter is going to a named person, then begin

Dear Mrs Sefton   Dear Mr Sefton

Dear Ms Sefton   Dear Miss Sefton

G

This is the main body of the letter. It might contain an opening statement about the reason for it being written, plus information, an explanation, questions, comments, requests, etc.

It is arranged in paragraphs.

It should be expressed in language that is right for the job and easy to understand.

H

Closing phrases = words to end off your letter.
These are also known as *complimentary closes* and *subscriptions*.

Endings are meant to match openings.
So . . . if you started with 'Dear Sir', 'Dear Madam' or 'Dear Sir/Madam', you should end with:

Yours faithfully,

If you are writing to a named person who you don't know or know only slightly, end with:

Yours sincerely   or   Yours truly

I

When you have completed your letter **write** your signature underneath your closing phrases like this:

Yours sincerely
Beverly Carson
(BEVERLEY CARSON MISS)

Always write your signature even if the letter is typed

J

Always print (or type) your name and title under your signature.

K

enc = enclosures.
These are things you have put in with your letter, such as, perhaps, a form or your birth certificate. Show how many things and what they are if that isn't already clear from the letter itself:

e.g. enc x 2 (Form BR12; birth certificate).

L

cc = carbon copies for other people.
These are more likely to be photocopies nowadays.
You may want the person you are writing to to know who else has received the same information.

If you *don't* . . . then don't show anything on your letter.

Some tips for writing business letters

With business and other important letters try to be:

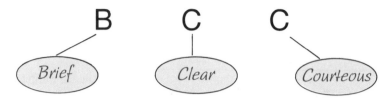

- Think about the length of your letter? Will someone bother to read it all?
- Think about the words you are using. Are they right for the job?
- Always try to keep sarcasm or anger in check.
- Try to be firm but polite in what you say and how you say it.

Compare these two letters:

Dear Sir,
     Today my Gas bill for the last quarter arrived and it was for £194.65. This is totally over the top! I live in a semi not the local Manor House.

Your office have obviously got it all wrong. Can't they work that computer? I want it sorted out and soon, so get someone onto it today.

        Yours faithfully,

Dear Sir,
     Usually, my quarterly Gas bill is round about £50, but the bill I received today was for £194.65.

I think there must have been some sort of computer error. Could you ask someone to look into the situation for me please?

I would appreciate a reply by return of post if at all possible as I am obviously anxious to sort matters out.

        Yours faithfully,

Which one is likely to get results quickly and co-operatively? Why?

Letters of complaint

These letters really follow the same guidelines as for general business letters except that they perhaps need more tact and care in how they are expressed. This can be difficult if you are feeling depressed or annoyed about something.

Before you write, give yourself time to **cool down.**

Perhaps ask someone else to read your draft through **before** you **commit** yourself to a final version.

Try replying to the following letter taking the information given underneath it *firmly* into account.

Day

Some Hope Insurances Ltd.

Night

Tel: Sparkbrook 2496

121-122 Burn Street,
Sparkbrook,
BIRMINGHAM
2PR 9QT
Tues. 5th May, 1989

Our Ref: 2CJK/194/80C

Dear Mr.

Re: <u>Your recent claim for compensation for a fire-destroyed leather coat</u>

We have now processed your claim and I have pleasure in enclosing a cheque for £19.95, which I hope you will find a reasonable compensation.

Yours faithfully,

RVick

(O.L.D. Nick (Mr.))
Area Manager

NOTE

Your coat, although fairly old, cost you £175 when you bought it four years ago; you have paid your premiums to this firm regularly over the years and never claimed for anything until now; also you have had to wait for two months for this claim to go through! You were hoping to get at least half of the original cost of the coat. How do you feel? I'll tell you . . .

outraged	*furious*	*let down*	*depressed*

but remember, be **brief, clear, courteous** (as far as you can!)

Job applications

Your first letter when applying for a job might be to ask for an application form or more details.

> Dear Sir,
>   I am writing with reference to the job of Office Supervisor in your Accounts Dept, which I saw advertised in this week's Citizen Newspaper.
>   I would be pleased if you would send me further details and an application form.
>   Yours faithfully,
>   Marion Tully.
>   (MARION TULLY MRS)

Helpful hints

Once you have the job details and have decided to apply, then your letter of application should follow a few guidelines:

- Collect your facts together first:

  - what skills does the job need?

  - what skills have you got?

  - what other information is required?

- Work out a rough draft.

- Start by saying who you are, why you are writing and where you saw or heard about the job.

- Give all relevant details – age, education, qualifications, other work experience.

- Bring out the good news about yourself in relation to the post you are applying for – why *you* would be good for the job. Don't be afraid to involve any part of your life experience and personality if it will help you to make the case for why you could do the job well.

- Don't let your letter ramble on – stick to the important points.

- Give referees who are unrelated to you and who you know will be happy to recommend you for the job.

Try writing a letter for Lorna keeping the above hints in mind:

CLERICAL POST
REGIONAL SPORTS CENTRE
Manor Road, Middleton M1 9UP

Person wanted for RECEPTION/TYPING work at this lively Centre.

Applicants should enjoy meeting the public, be able to type at a reasonable speed, organise rotas, deal with bookings and records, handle some small fee collection duties.

£90 per week. 37 hours.

Apply in writing to:
Centre Manager, John Dunn

Facts about Lorna

Age 33   Non-smoker   Divorced
Two children (10yrs/7yrs)   Drives/clean licence
Hobbies: Gardening/Sewing/TV/Badminton

Hasn't worked outside the home for 9 years. Is secretary to her local Residents' Association. Has done some voluntary work in her children's school. Got typing certificate at 16 years. Worked switchboard, reception and typing for 7 years from leaving school to starting her family. Likes people. Has two weeks holiday booked for August.

Referee: Mrs Fisher, Headmistress, Ladywell Jr School, Middleton MP9 9UP

Memos

You may find you have to write messages at work. In some jobs there may be a need to write 'memos'.

MEMORANDUM	MEMO	MEMORANDA
singular	abbreviation	plural

A memo is a short note sent between people at work.

Usually firms have their own in-house memo forms. Memos are normally handwritten and a reply may be written on the bottom or on the back.

A memo might look something like this:

From: *Mrs Turner*   To: *Full time Tutors*
Dept: *Education*   Dept: *Maths*
Date: *29. 6. 89*   Tel. Ext: *294*

Subject: *Resource Requests*

Please note that all Resource Requests must be made using form RQ1, available from the Admin Dept. Pass all completed RQ1's to me

Signed: *Annie Turner (Deputy)*

> You don't need 'Dear . . .'

> or 'Yours . . .'

A memo should:

- say who it is *from* and who it is *to*
- have a *date*
- have a *title*
- only be about one thing: it's *not* a letter.

Writing a reference

**A referee should not be a relation of the applicant.
A referee is expected to speak favourably of the applicant.**

When you write a letter of reference for someone:

1. Explain your connection with, and experience of, the person who has given your name and say how long you have known them.

2. Describe the qualities, skills and experience the person has that you feel are important to the job or role being considered.

3. Express confidence in the person's ability to carry out the job or role well.

4. Offer an invitation for further contact and discussion.

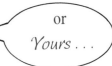 **NOTE**

- Don't agree to write a reference for someone you can't honestly be positive about. Bad references might land you in court.

- If you are the referee simply because you are the person's current or last employer and you have nothing good to say, then just give the barest information: e.g.

Miss .... worked for us as a .... from ....

.... to .... She left on ....

Such a short note would probably speak for itself!

When you are writing letters think about:

- Who you are writing to . . . and . . . why? (**audience** and **purpose**)
- What do you want to know or tell them?
- What sort of letter or reply is expected?
- What is the timescale for replying?
- What information is needed? And where is it?
- Are there specific questions to be answered?
- What will you include? What will you exclude?
- What sort of tone should your letter adopt?
- Will you draft it first?
- When and where are you going to write the letter?
- Do you need to keep a copy?

Books

40 Letters to Write, Andrew Fergus (Hulton Education, 1979).

Send a Friend a Letter: Workbook for Students of Letter-writing (Scottish Community Education Council, 1987).

1. Think of 3 people you know and address an envelope for each. Mark one as confidential.

2. Quickly jot down 10 things you might talk about in a letter to a friend, based on the last 2 weeks of your life.

3. You want to take out a £6000 bank loan. The money is to buy a computer to develop the setting up of your own plumbing business. You need the loan over 3 years. The monthly repayments are £150. Write a letter to your uncle (Mr John Clements of 19 Bloom Avenue, Stapleford, Lancs ST6 5PR) asking him if he will agree to be your guarantor.

4. Design a basic letter that could be used over and over again for use whenever a child has had to have time off school. Just leave gaps for the changes in details such as reason, date, etc.

5. A work-mate is in hospital out of town. He has had a serious operation and may never be able to return to work. Write him a letter that will cheer him up a bit and keep him in touch without making him anxious.

6. You work in the Sales Department of a large firm. The strip lighting keeps flickering. Write a memo to Mrs Andrews in Maintenance to report this and ask for action.

Forms and form-filling

Look at the following statements about forms.
Decide which are *true* and which are *false*.
Put ☐T or ☐F in the box
next to each statement.

Full Name _____
Address _____
_____
_____
Tel. No _____
Date of Birth _____

Forms are designed:

1. To annoy and confuse people.	
2. To collect information in a set way.	
3. To speed up the process of collecting and assessing information.	
4. To make selection easier.	
5. To help with making decisions.	
6. To make a reply to a form-filler faster.	
7. To act as a record.	
8. To (in some cases) act as a legal document.	

Probably you should have put a ☐T in all the boxes except number 1, although it might not always feel that way!

Unfortunately forms do seem to turn some people off, make some people worry, and even make some people angry.

I haven't time to do this form!

what do I put down?

forms bore me to death

I don't understand the words

what do I leave out?

will they know what I mean?

BUT ...

Forms are a part of almost everyone's life. As a very specific *means of communication* they are worth thinking about.

REMEMBER

- Not all forms are very complicated.

- Most forms want information that's *short* and *to the point*.

- You need to understand the *purpose* of any particular form and the *meaning* of the words it uses, in order to fill it in properly.

- A form that's filled in thoughtfully and clearly is more likely to get *good results quickly*.

Where do forms crop up?

Everywhere and all the time! But they range from the simple to the impossible depending on their purpose and who designs them.

Have you ever completed a form for any of these reasons?

Tick ✔ for YES:	X for NO:	Put a ? by any you don't understand	
For medical purposes		For state benefits	
To get a personal loan		For tax purposes	
To get a passport		Mail Order	
For library membership		College enrolment	
To get a season ticket		Holiday bookings	
Pools coupons		For school	
Union membership		To attend a course	
Accident report		To claim money	
To send off for 'freebies'		Work stock orders	
To get a driving licence		Work phone messages	
To register a vehicle		Annual leave requests	

If you have ticked most things . . . you know the score!

If you have mostly put an X or a ? then you have probably still got a lot to experience about forms.

Two different form-filling situations

No. 1

> You mean you want me to fill in this form now? Right away? While you wait?

Filling in a form 'on the spot' can be a very threatening situation, especially if someone watches over you whilst you do it! So it's a good idea to carry with you a *personal information memo* for quick reference and reassurance.

No. 2

> Oh, I see. I can take this form home with me and let you have it back in a few days. Great! Can I have an extra copy please?

Wow! What a relief and what an opportunity.

Question? How can this situation help the form-filler?

Answer It gives the form-filler *time* to get *organised*.

Getting organised

Having time to complete a form means:

- you can arrange things so as to allow time to do the job well
- you can read through the form (and any related notes) properly before you start
- you can collect together information not readily to hand
- you can sort out unfamiliar words and their meaning
- you can do a rough draft first
- you can ask someone to check what you've done if you want to
- you can find a pen that suits you – a black ink pen if possible
- you can adapt your handwriting to the space on the form
- you can make a copy, or photocopy, of the completed form for yourself.

Next time you have to fill in a form it might be worth looking at this list again.

Either try making yourself a *personal information memo* from scratch, *or* adapt the example below.

Example:

PERSONAL INFORMATION MEMO

Personal Information

Christian Names/Forenames/First Names _____

Surname/Family name _____

Marital Status _____ Date of Birth _____ Day _____ Month _____ Year _____

OR __/__/__   OR ⟋⟋⟋⟋⟋⟋

Present Address _____

_____

_____

_____ Post Code _____

Home Tel. No. _____ Work Tel. No. _____

Nationality _____ Place of Birth _____

Next of Kin _____ Relationship _____

Name of Spouse _____

Full names of children and dates of birth _____

(in chronological order) _____

_____

_____

_____

Important References

Work/Employee Number _____ National Insurance No. _____

Child Benefit Number _____ Blood Group _____

Other Important References

Car Registration _____ Own weight _____ Own height _____

Education Note down schools, etc., dates and any exams taken/passed

Work history

Dates – from – to	Firm/Organisation	Nature of job

Language on forms

Some words on forms are old fashioned, some are technical, some are legal – many are unfamiliar in daily life. Some words ask for information and some give instructions. You'll also find that words for the same thing may vary from form to form.

Can you match up these words from forms with their meaning?

Use a dictionary if you are not sure . . . or ask someone.

1. alien
2. guarantor
3. employer
4. employee
5. guardian
6. naturalised
7. referee
8. designation or status
9. next of kin
10. spouse
11. batchelor
12. spinster
13. distinguishing features
14. physical disability
15. for office use or official use only
16. position applied for
17. annual subscription
18. nominated by
19. authorise
20. current
21. particulars
22. institution
23. liable for
24. witnessed by
25. qualifications

Answers:
1d, 2r, 3h, 4s, 5t, 6l, 7x, 8i, 9e, 10j, 11s,
12a, 13v, 14q, 15b, 16m, 17u, 18w, 19c,
20n, 21k, 22o, 23y, 24p, 25f.

a) an unmarried woman

b) do not write in this space

c) give permission

d) foreigner

e) person most closely related to you by birth or marriage

f) skills/tests/certificate gained

g) the worker

h) the boss/firm you work for

i) Could be Mr, Mrs, Miss, Ms, or single, widowed, divorced, separated or the job you do e.g. housewife, supervisor

j) person married to you

k) details/facts

p) signed in the presence of

l) not born British but having become a British citizen

n) now

r) the person prepared to guarantee your regular repayments

q) an illness or disability such as epilepsy, deafness or a limp

m) the job you want to be considered for

o) school/college/university

u) amount to be paid each year

v) marks on body e.g. a scar, which can identify you

s) an unmarried man

t) someone who looks after a child in the place of parents

x) someone who knows you well and who will comment on your suitability and character

y) responsible for

w) put forward by

More form-filling tips

- Answer the questions in order.
- If a question doesn't apply to you put N/A in the space. (N/A means not applicable. An empty space may mean your form will be returned).
- Check you have answered all questions on *both* sides of the form.
- If there is a large space for some personal information, draft out what you want to say first and then copy it onto the form.
- If there is only a small space for something you want to say more about, write on a separate piece of paper and state what you have done on the form, e.g. 'Q.7 See attached letter'.

Look at the following example of a form completed by Barbara Ross. See what you can learn or confirm from it and what else it prompts you to find out more about.

APPLICATION FOR EMPLOYMENT	Post PART-TIME: CLERICAL RECEPTION	Please complete this form in BLOCK LETTERS

Christian Names/Forenames: BARBARA ANN   Sex: M (F) Circle one

Surname/Last Name: ROSS   Date of Birth: 2.3.57

Home Address: 14 DROVERS ROAD LANGRAVE

Town: HITCHIN   Post Code: LA6 2PR

County: HERTS.   Home Tel. No: HITCHIN 29416   Work Tel. No: N/A

Marital Status: ~~Married~~/Single/Widowed/~~Divorced~~/~~Separated~~ *Delete as appropriate

Maiden Name: GREEN   Nationality: BRITISH

Name of Spouse (if alive): N/A   Place of Birth: EDINBURGH

Next of Kin: MRS. JOAN GREEN   Relationship: MOTHER

Address: FLAT 2B, MORTON CLOSE GLASGOW G16 4UX.   Tel. No: 0643 - 927184

Number of Children: (Give ages in chronological order): 2 — 6½ YEARS AND 9 YRS.

Leisure Interests: I LIKE READING, KNITTING, T.V., GARDENING AND I HELP AT A LOCAL PLAYSCHOOL.

Education: (Schools/Colleges/Dates/Examinations passed/certificates gained):

MIRFIELD HIGH EDINBURGH	1908-73	CSE: ART, MATHS, GEOGRAPHY G.C.E: ENGLISH LITERATURE ENGLISH LANGUAGE

Current Employment	Position	Name/Address of Employer
NONE	N/A	N/A

Previous Employment

Employer	Position Held	Dates	Reasons for Leaving	Salary or Wage
CALEDONIAN BISCUIT CO. ASCOT ROAD (ED.9)	MACHINE SUPERVISOR	1972 - 1979	TO START MY FAMILY	£60.p.wk.

Name of a Referee: JOHN McDAID (DOCTOR)

Address: 11 BLOSSOM COURT, LANGRAVE, HITCHIN

Position Held: DOCTOR   Tel. No: HITCHIN 94006

Signature of Applicant: B.A. Ross.   Date: 9.6.89

Next time you fill in a form, bear these key points in mind:

- **Read** it all the way through before you start writing
- **Gobbledegook** – be sure you really know what those words mean
- **Think** of the implications:
- **Draft** – don't rush into using ink
- **Accurate** – see that your information is correct, no questions missed out, no enclosures forgotten.
- **Your records** – keep a copy of important forms or at least note down what you wrote.

ASSIGNMENT

Pick up forms whenever you see them, just to glance through for new words or unusual layouts. The Post Office has a wide range of forms to practise on. Call in and collect some. Or you could collect examples from the list on p.46.

Notes

This section looks at *notes*, not the ones you scribble for the milkman, your family or to pass on a quick message at work, but structured, organised *notes*.

Making notes is about:

- clear thinking
- getting things down quickly
- using structure and order

Making notes is a good way of jotting down things we have:

seen or heard . . .   *radio, TV, a talk, a meeting, telephone call, accident witnessed.*

read . . .   *poster, advert, book, timetable, magazine, newspaper, study material.*

thought of . . .   *ideas, plans for projects, activities, letters, essays, things to remember.*

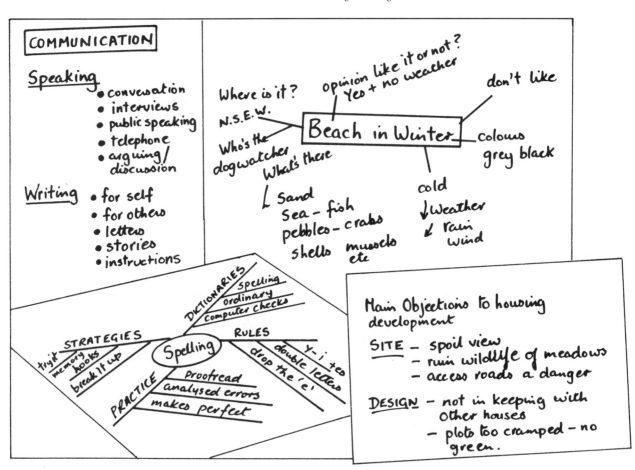

Anyone can use notes whenever there is a need to get things down *briefly* and in a *structured* way.

 Good notes are ⬚short⬚ and ⬚organised.⬚

Making notes can be useful in several ways.
Look at the following paragraph about the benefits of making notes.
Compare this with the 2 examples below which are in note form.

WHY USE NOTES?

Notes are useful for several reasons. Firstly, when we make notes we have to think carefully and this helps us to understand the subject. Secondly, notes are a short useful record which can be looked back on later. This revision helps our memory. Thirdly, it has been shown that students who use notes do much better than those who do not. They learn the subject more quickly and do better in exams.

A

WHY USE NOTES?

1. THEY MAKE YOU THINK
– helps understanding
– keeps you interested
– helps structured thinking

2. THEY ARE A SHORT RECORD
– useful to look back at
– helps memory

3. GOOD FOR STUDY
– to learn the subject
– to pass exams

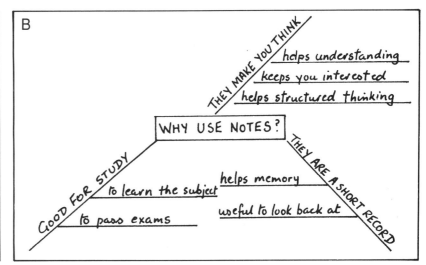

A is in *lines*.
These are called *linear notes*.

B is in a pattern.
These are called *patterned notes* (or sometimes 'spidergrams').

These are the 2 most common ways of making notes

If you are happier working in LINES you may prefer LINEAR NOTES.

If you like shape and (PATTERN) you may prefer (PATTERNED NOTES.)

. . . or you may develop a new style of your own.

REMEMBER

There isn't *one* way or a *best* way of making notes.

You should use any way that suits *you*, depending on:

- your purpose
- the subject
- your mood
- the amount of time you have

Tips for making notes

- Think of the *main points/ideas*.

- Try to get all the details linked to a main idea (and in order of importance).

- Allow plenty of space; you may want to add things later.

- Use a highlighter pen (most stationers sell these) to mark the main points.

- Practise making notes while watching TV or listening to discussions on the radio.

- Listen for the main meaning and write down words, not sentences.

- If you ever help others (adults or children) with their study, at any level, show them how to use notes. This will help *you* to develop your skill and it will help *them* to improve their study skills for the future.

Making notes from a piece of reading

For this assignment you need a piece of text. It can be from a book on any subject, a newspaper or magazine article, a report or document from work or something you are studying.

1. Take a page or a paragraph of text and read it for *the main points*. You may find a highlighter pen useful for this.

2. Make some notes on the main points and then add the minor points or other details. You can use one of the methods below to make your notes or use your own style, or you might like to try both methods and see which you prefer.

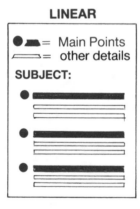

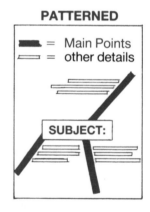

If you often make notes, you have probably already found a way which suits you. Perhaps this section has given you some new ideas.

If you haven't tried making notes before, this section may have helped you to think about how notes could be useful for you (at home/work/study).

It is important when making notes to:

- **Listen** for main points
- **Read** for main points
- **Think** of main ideas

Then you can add the details.

Don't forget good notes are **short** and **organised.**

Personal writing

Personal writing is not for everyone. You don't *need* to be good at it (unless it is part of your study course or job).

But many people enjoy this way of writing and it can be a good way of developing your writing skills.

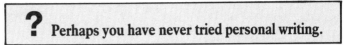

? Perhaps you have never tried personal writing.

If you enjoy any of the following or would like to try them, then this section is for you.

- Writing from personal experience
- Writing to give your opinion
- Writing short stories

If none of these appeal to you, have a quick look through to see if anything catches your eye, and then move onto another section.

Writing from personal experience

This can be a very satisfying way to write. Some people say it helps to 'get things off your chest', or to recapture events that have passed. You can write just for yourself or for others to read. You might like to think about some of these:

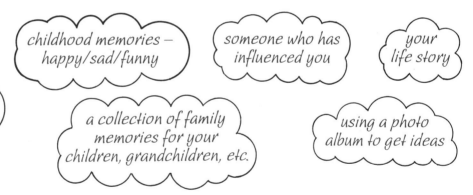

- childhood memories – happy/sad/funny
- someone who has influenced you
- your life story
- comparing your childhood with those of children today
- a collection of family memories for your children, grandchildren, etc.
- using a photo album to get ideas

You could also read other people's memories, life stories, diaries, etc. Public libraries usually have a good collection of these.

Things to bear in mind when writing from personal experience

- An experience could be 50 years ago or 5 minutes ago!
- Some things may be too personal for others to read.
- If it is a personal diary (for your eyes only) you can write how you like.
- Writing your whole life story can be a big task; start with a part of it.
- If you are writing for others, it has to be interesting.
- If you mention other people by name, make sure they won't mind!
- You could collect your experiences on tape and write them up later (or get someone else to write them up for you).

I tell myself
over and over again
"SNAP OUT OF IT"
But,
on days like these.
I do not know myself.
I am a stranger
to myself,
on days like these........

I was born in a wooden cottage
in a small village in Essex on
13th October 1939, the second born
of eight. The seventh girl died
as a baby. My earliest mem...

Durham 50 years ago.

The hardship of the miners' strike and the lack
of money is knitting the community more
tightly together. The people that you would least
expect to help are proving to be the most
helpful. I think this spirit of friendship and
helpfulness must be something like the
war-time days. Perhaps some good will come out
of the hardship; perhaps this community spirit
will outlast the strike.

It was a messy divorce, most of
them are. The most painful part
was explaining to the children
that we ... still loved them
but didn't love each other
anymore. Several times I
thought that making the break
was going to be harder than
living with an unhappy marriage
but that's something you can
never be sure of.

...front of the pictu...
...stones 50 years ago.
...m sets. There were
...there were hors...
...My father had an ol...
...He sold fruit and ...
...were well-made
...pull very well. Y...
...share them up h...
...handle to get them sta...

...wished that he could get gold
stars at school. One day he came
home with a gold star in his
book. I said, "you see it is worth
working hard to get a star". He
said, "I found it and stuck it in
myself".

Writing to give your opinion

In conversation it's easy to say

If you want my opinion . . .

But when we put our opinions or views in writing it is usually for a more important *purpose* than casual comment. It becomes a permanent record in writing, so we need to:

- be careful how we 'phrase' it
- make sure we've thought about **purpose** and **audience.**
- be prepared to work at it – (see p.30) **edit/proofread**

So that is *says what we want it to* and *with our own 'voice'* but in writing.

The Local Residents' Association object
most strongly to the new development.
We feel that is should not go ahead, for
the following reasons:

1. It is against the local policy plan
because it involves new house in
open countryside.
2. The roads couldn't cope with the
traffic.
3. The design of the houses is not in
keeping with the rest of the village.
4. Local residents feel that too many
new houses have been built in the
past 3 years.

(300 signatures to this effect are
enclosed).

Things to bear in mind when writing opinions

- sound convincing by using the best words (see p.7 on using a dictionary/thesaurus)
- plan and structure the piece of writing (Notes may help – p.50)
- back up your statements with examples and evidence to sound convincing
- don't keep repeating the same point; it will weaken your argument
- don't let your strong feelings make you write in an offensive way or people won't read it.

I believe that people
take too many pills.
I wonder if we would
need so many if doctors
had the time to talk
to patients instead of
rushing to write out
a prescription and
then.... "next patient please".

I feel I must complain about the
unsightly litter which is spoiling
the city centre. I believe that this
is making our city less attractive
to tourists. The city council is
very keen to promote an image
of clean, historic beauty but it
should give equal attention to
ensuring that it lives up to this
image.

I admit that smoking
is a bad habit. I know
it is a health risk and
expensive too. But I
don't drink alcohol, nor
do I drive a car which
produces poisonous gas
nor do I ever do
anything to cause harm
to anyone. So please
allow me just one vice
without making me
feel like an outcast

When you are reading others' opinions, notice what sounds convincing, clearly written and easy to follow. Try to use the same techniques when you give *your* opinions in writing.

Writing short stories

Short stories can be fun to write, whether they are for children or adults. A short story can be a few pages, one page, or even a few lines, as in the mini-saga below.

> **The reason on the 8.10 am**
>
> Twenty years with the railways.
> Bill really enjoyed his work.
> Being illiterate hadn't mattered, although Mary nagged him to learn.
> Today as the 8.10 am arrived, Bill waited to help.
>
> A deaf, blind man approached.
> "How can I find this address?
> Please write in my hand."
> Bill stiffened. Mary had won.

For a short story to be good it needs:

- a setting (place)

- characters (people/animals, etc.)

- storyline (something must *happen*)

Think of the first stories we hear as children; fairy tales, folk tales, etc. Think of some of your favourites. Most of them have a *setting*, *characters* and a *storyline*.

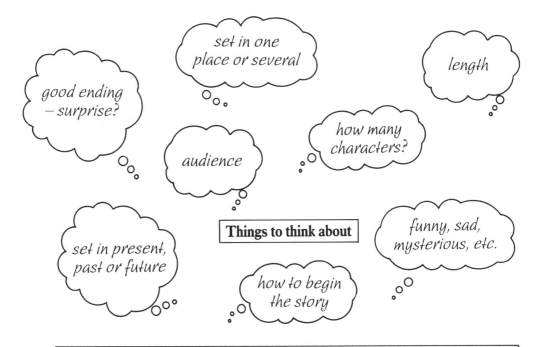

good ending – surprise?

set in one place or several

length

audience

how many characters?

Things to think about

funny, sad, mysterious, etc.

set in present, past or future

how to begin the story

The 3-word Starter Method

This can be a useful way to get started with writing a short story.

1. Look at the words opposite
2. Choose any 3 words.
3. Try to link them in a story.
4. Before you start, take time to think and jot down a few ideas.
5. Try to keep the story short.
6. Try to think of a good ending.

Remember

- setting
- characters
- storyline

child   camera   place   campsite
telephone   keys   pilot
pilot   café   doll   newspaper
photograph   dry cleaners
knife   pub
dentist   racecourse   garden   radio
necklace   steps   waitress   taxi
scientist   river   allotment
clock   rosebush   lift   circus
suitcase   briefcase   hospital

Reading skills

This section looks at developing good reading skills.

What do you think good reading is?

		✓ YES	✗ NO
A	*Always reading every word*		
	Saying the words in your head		
C	*Always understanding every word*		
D	*Reading carefully at all times*		

- If you said **no** for each one, you already understand a lot about good reading skills.

- If you said **yes** for any of them, you may find this section interesting to read.

There are *times* when you need to read carefully word by word and understand everything (forms, technical writing, legal documents, etc).

There are *times*, too, when it is good to hear the words in your head – or even say them aloud – to appreciate the meaning and sounds (poetry, some descriptive writing, or things written in dialect or accents).

But if you use A B C or D all the time you are not helping your reading.

Let's take each point in turn:

A	Reading word by word is slow. This can be boring and then we can't be bothered to read or we don't remember what we've read.

B	Hearing the words in your head slows you down. It can also confuse you because your eye is moving on ahead while you are still hearing the words further back down the line.

C	We can usually get by without understanding every word. Most good readers guess what is meant and often mentally substitute another word without losing meaning.

D	It would be very boring to have to read *everything* carefully. Imagine reading newspapers, magazines, posters, adverts, etc., carefully. It would be hard work, slow and *boring*.

Reasons for reading

Good readers read in different ways . . . for different reasons.

 *Think* ○○ about some of your reasons for reading.

Do they include any from this list?

	✓
For **entertainment** – magazines, stories, novels, jokes, etc.	
To **learn** about a subject – for hobbies or study	
To **find** a particular piece of **information** – e.g. telephone number	
To **follow instructions** – forms, recipes, DIY furniture	
To **pass the time** – browse notices, adverts, newspapers, cereal packets	
To **collect information** – for work, study, home	
To **decide** quickly about something – e.g. junk mail	
To **prepare** for an event – meeting, interview, going on holiday	

Each of these reading tasks has a *purpose* which suggests a way or *method* of reading.

Which way is best?

There isn't a best way – only different ways, each suitable for its purpose.

You may already use different reading methods, without realising what they are called. That's good.

If you always read everything in the same way, this section may be helpful for you.

Reading methods

There are 4 main methods of reading:

Scanning

Skimming

Light reading (sometimes called *normal* reading)

Careful reading (sometimes called *intensive* reading)

We nearly always use a mixture of these when we read, but let's look at each one separately to see their *purpose*.

Scanning

Purpose: To look for something

- *Scanning* is the quickest method of 'reading'. It's a bit like a scan in a hospital. We ignore most of the words because we know what we are looking for and we usually have an idea of where to find it. Our eyes move quickly, sweeping over the page or the text.

- *Scanning* is a functional way of reading – to get things done.

Finding a Word in a Dictionary

Using a bus or train timetable.

Using a Telephone Directory

Checking TV programme times.

Using an index at the back of a book.

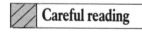 **Skimming**

Purpose: To get the general idea

- *Skimming* is fast reading to get a surface view. It's a bit like skimming stones on water; you don't want to go too deep.

- When we *skim*-read we don't read every word. We try to take in words, phrases, headings, illustrations and anything which will help us to get the general idea.

- A lot of adult reading is *skimming*. We *skim* through magazines, newspapers and books to see what they contain. We are not looking for anything in particular but if we do find something interesting, we may stop to read it in more detail.

Light reading

Purpose: To read for interest or pleasure

- *Light reading* is the normal, fairly quick, way we read. It is often by choice and we do not worry too much about concentrating, understanding every word or remembering what we've read.

- We use *light reading* for magazine or newspaper articles, stories and novels, jokes, letters from friends or family and anything which is not of great seriousness or depth of meaning.

- *Light reading* is the most natural and often the most enjoyable way of reading.

Careful reading

Purpose: To read for understanding or for study

- *Careful reading* or intensive reading is a slower and more serious method of reading. This doesn't necessarily mean reading each word slowly, but we may need to re-read some parts to get real understanding.

- *Careful reading* is all about *understanding*, *remembering* and really *thinking* about what we read (being critical). It's very different from the other methods.

- We use *careful reading* for: official letters, study material, legal documents, forms and instructions and complicated texts.

Sometimes when we read these things we read the words out loud slowly – it seems to help our understanding of very complicated reading material. Page 65 has more information on reading for study.

 You may have noticed that the methods of reading have different speeds:

NOTE

 scan
very fast

 skim
fast

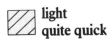 light
quite quick

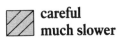 careful
much slower

ASSIGNMENTS

1. Scanning

This is an exercise in looking for information by **scanning.**

- Scanning is the *fastest* method
- You don't read everything carefully
- You pass your eyes over the text

What to do:

1. Quickly scan each text to find the information asked for.
2. Circle or underline it when you find it.
3. Move onto the next text.
4. Finish all texts before you check your time.

Write your start time here ....

How much ginger do you need?

(Red split lentils with cabbage)

Ingredients:

7	ounces red split lentils
10	ounces of white cabbage
2	pints water
½	teaspoon turmeric
1	teaspoon cumin seeds
1½	teaspoons fresh ginger
2-4	cloves of garlic
1½	teaspoons salt
5	tablespoons oil
4	ounces tomato

Who does First Aid?

Name	Department	Tel. Ext.
JAN ADAMS	SWITCHBOARD	100
DAVID BROWN	MAINTENANCE	240
PAULINE BRUCE	WAGES	135
D.K. CROSS	TRANSPORT	221
W. DODDS	SECURITY	139
BILL EVANS	MAINTENANCE	249
CHRIS FARSSI	TYPING POOL	215
SUE HIBBERD	CANTEEN	124
N.R. KHAN	SECURITY	139
JOHN MORRIS	FIRST AID	214
J.T. THOMAS	SWITCHBOARD	100
ELSIE WATTS	TYPING POOL	215

When did the writer join the RAF?

In between times since I left school, I had been going to the youth employment office trying to get into the Air Force. I had filled in the application when I was sixteen and it seemed like years before I heard anything. Then one day I got a letter asking me to go for a consideration test in Ipswich I didn't know what to expect but I had a feeling that I wouldn't make it. It turned out to be a few sums and some puzzles. I know now that they were initiative tests. I was finally sworn in to the R.A.F. on June 19th 1957. For the first week I felt as if I was living in dream. I didn't think I would make it but now I was in and on the same level as the other girls No-one here new that I was from such a large family. We were all feeling a bit homesick but determined to make it. I went on to become an orderly and then a stewardess, working in the officers' mess.

Finish time ....   Time taken ....

How did you do?

More than 3 minutes		You could speed up with regular practice
Between 1 - 2 minutes		You have a reasonable scanning speed
Less than 1 minute		You are a skilled scanner!

2. Skimming

This exercise is about reading to get the general idea by **skimming** the text.

Remember:

- Skimming is going over the surface quickly
- You don't stop to read in depth
- Use clues to help you – headings, layout, keywords, diagrams, pictures.

What to do:

1. Skim-read each text quickly.

2. Decide what it is about.

3. Write the letter in the box at the bottom which matches the text.

4. Do all texts before you check your time.

These texts have no clues – so you *need* to skim-read.

Write your start time here ....

A

We do not claim to have all the answers to the country's problems. We do not think that the other parties have them either. However, the PKN Party truly believes that it has the policies to start to make this country a better place for everyone. Whatever your age, belief or life-style, you can be sure that by voting for the PKN Party, you will be saying yes to the following policies:

B

Sun Valley has many indoor activities for both adults and children. If the weather is bad your holiday isn't ruined; there's always something to enjoy in one of our pavilions. Sunny Valley is the ideal holiday centre for all the family. Why not treat the family to a real holiday this year?

C

Mrs Barton was very helpful, almost too helpful. She said that it was her night for bingo and she never got home until 11.00 pm. On the night in question she said that she arrived home at 11.00 pm to find the dead body on the kitchen floor. However, her neighbour had seen her leaving the house in a great hurry at 10.30 pm. Things were not looking good for Mrs Barton.

D

Several members of staff have asked for information about the new arrangements for Sick Pay. There are leaflets available but to allow you to ask questions, I have arranged for a short meeting to be held on Monday 3rd February at 4.30 pm. Will members of staff please let me know if they intend to come to the meeting so that I can arrange for Mrs Tyson to provide refreshments.

☐ healthy eating   ☐ staff meeting on Sick Pay

☐ detective story   ☐ election leaflet

☐ complaint letter   ☐ holiday brochure

Finish time ....   Time taken ....

How did you do?

More than 3 minutes		You would benefit from regular practice
Between 2 - 3 minutes		Your skimming is quite good
Less than 2 minutes		You have very good skimming skills

If you have completed this section on Reading skills you should:

- Know about the 4 methods
- Have a good idea when to use them

This will make you a more *efficient* reader and a more *skilful* reader.

Check your knowledge of reading skills
(look back if you are not sure)

Scanning is used for ....

Skimming is used for ....

Light reading is used for ....

Careful reading is used for ....

We nearly always use a mixture of methods when we read.

If you think you need to improve your *reading skills*, start by making a *decision* to take *control of your reading*.

You can do this by:

- Thinking about why you are reading something – **purpose**
- Deciding how to read it *(skim, scan, light, careful reading* or a mixture).

and also by:

- Thinking about whether something is *worth* reading or not
- Sometimes rejecting things that are badly written or badly presented (if you have the choice!)

Reading beyond the words

There's more to reading than meets the eye!

This is literally quite true. We need to look *beyond the words*.

> Much of what we understand from what we read isn't actually stated. We read sense into words using our own knowledge, experience and preferences. Have you ever been amazed at a television version of a book you've read? Different people . . . different pictures!

What do we use to build meaning into reading?

- *The context can help:* Here's a number – 020489. Is it a telephone number? A prisoner's number? A house number. An order number? A couple of these possibilities you could knock out because the number is neither long enough nor short enough. Now try seeing it on an invoice in a column marked 'date'. Got it?

- *Pictures, illustrations, photographs and diagrams* are a fast way of defining some characters and places, or a sense of history or atmosphere, or relationships. Children use pictures a lot. Adults often like them too. If you get a book with lots of pictures or photos in it do you look at these first? Most people do. It helps you get into the meaning quickly.

- *Clues in the written text:* Question marks, exclamation marks, dots, dashes, bold type, italics, spaces. All kinds of punctuation can help readers to feel and hear loudness, softness, anxiety, anger . . . any number of moods and emotions.

- *Inference (drawing conclusions from general information):*

John, Alan and Tiny were trying to relax. They lazed under the tropical trees and took little notice of the car which stopped next to their tents. Then they recognised Bill, the Londoner who was driving. Bill stepped out and held the car door open.

As Royston emerged the three men sprang to their feet and stood stiffly to attention . . .

Are the men soldiers?

Are they abroad?

Are they British?

Is Royston strict?

Is Royston an Officer?

You are likely to be pretty certain in your own mind about the answers to these questions, but not from direct facts. Think about how it's been done and the part your own experience played in the process.

- *Making the most of the information you are given:* Solve this problem. You have all the facts you need.

> *A farmer has to take a dog, a duck and some corn across a river. His boat can only carry himself and one other thing across at a time. He can't leave the dog alone with the duck. He can't leave the duck with the corn. How can the farmer manage to end up with himself and the rest safely on the other side in 7 journeys?*

- *Making sense out of gobbledegook:* This example is from an insurance endorsement relating to a broken windscreen replacement:

> The entitlement of the Insured to No Claim Discount under Section 5 (No Claim Discount) hereof shall not be prejudiced by any claim for the breakage of the windscreen or windows of the Insured car provided always that no other payment is made by the Underwriters in respect of damage to the Insured car except for the scratching of the bodywork surrounding the broken windscreen or windows and resulting from such breakage.

Well! It's possible to get a feel for what it means, but difficult to get a real grip on it without help or some very specialist knowledge. Sometimes the words are there, but the meaning is outside of our experience.

- *Not taking words and pictures at face value:* Adverts are a good example of a reading situation where readers must take notice of persuasive language and images; of presentations that can fool you; of promises that aren't really there.

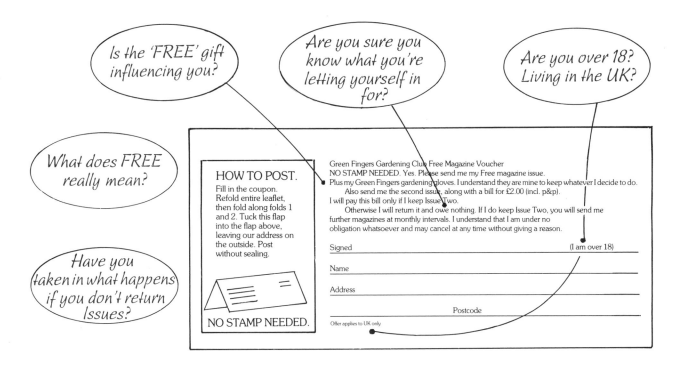

- *Hearing the writer's 'voice':* Bias, unweighted arguments or deliberate attempts to sell you a particular view of things arise all the time in writing. Just because it's in print doesn't mean it's *true!* Read between the lines. Think about how some words limit you or channel you, how they start to make you see things one way. Who is the writer? Have they a personal axe to grind? Maybe it's not always deliberate, but it needs *challenging* anyway.

'ALL THE Daddies on the bus go read, read . . .
All the Mummies on the bus go chatter, chatter, chatter . . .'
Song taught in nursery school.

What images of women are being reinforced here?

'A 32-YEAR-OLD Paddock Wood man who beat up his wife during a row at their home was given a conditional discharge by Tunbridge Wells magistrates last week. He was told that had the victim not been his wife the penalty might have been more severe.'
Kent and Sussex Courier

REPORT: July 6th 1988: John Smith reported 1st Aid Room 10am – lacerated right hand. Says safety shield slipped and fell on feed tray. Says shield loose for some time. Wishes to claim compensation. Foreman says machine inspected previous week. No faults noted. All employees should report faults immediately. Smith well known for carelessness. Regular absentee, unco-operative. Already had warning about possible dismissal.

And . . .

Question?
Does John Smith really stand a fair chance based on this report?

- *Not accepting things that don't make sense:* In the following few sentences 8 things don't add up. Maybe the writer's a bad proofreader . . . or in a hurry . . . but it's not good enough!

Mr and Mrs Jones and their son, 19 year-old Alan, were off to Birmingham to stay with some friends for the weekend. Early that Wednesday morning the four of them loaded the car and left Watford, heading south along the motorway. They hoped to reach their Uncle's for about 9pm. Traffic was really heavy and Mr and Mrs James shared the driving. Anna couldn't help as she was still too young to have passed her driving test. She just sat there at the back of the van, reading.

Reading is a **responsibility.** It is far more than just recognising words and doing so at different speeds for different purposes. It involves:

- **Constructing meaning**
- **Making sense**
- **Using judgement**
- **Drawing conclusions**

Readers always need to be aware of the writer's 'voice' and the effect of their own bias and experience on what they are reading.

ASSIGNMENTS

1. Compare 2 articles from 2 different newspapers about *the same topic,* in terms of language, facts, images, emphasis and so on.

2. Find a book with plenty of illustrations. Think about how the pictures add or take away from that book for you and why.

3. Try writing something, e.g. about Mrs Thatcher, from several different viewpoints – from your own, Neil Kinnock's, her daughter's, her baby grandson's . . .

Reading to learn

A student who joined an adult education class was determined to learn to read. After 2 years she was reading quite well. She decided to start reading books about her hobby (breeding rabbits).

She is no longer

LEARNING to read

but has started

READING to learn

This section is about using reading skills to study or to learn.

Hairdressing   Car maintenance   Office skills   Home decorating

Sociology   Bee-keeping   Catering   Hotel management

Computing   Gardening   Lace-making   Business studies   Origami

Whatever subject you are studying, you will probably need to use a mixture of all 4 reading methods:

 Scanning    **Skimming**   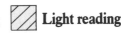 **Light reading**    **Careful reading**

These methods are explained on page 57

But the one you will use most is the last one: **careful reading.**

When we study a subject, we usually rely on what we can read about it in books (and sometimes what we hear people say). The problem is that there are usually many books on the subject and some are more useful to us than others.

Deciding which books are good and *getting the information* that we need from them quickly is a *study skill*.

Reading and study skills

There are lots of books on how to study; you can borrow them from libraries or buy them. However, you could spend hours studying books on 'How to Study'!

Basically, there are a few simple steps you can take to help you to *read for study* more easily and quickly.

1. Find the *best* book(s).
2. Check that it's *worth reading.*
3. Read only the *parts* you need.
4. Make good *notes* of what you read (see on Notes on p.50)
5. Keep a *record* of the book(s) you used.

Five simple steps to good study reading

1. Find the best book(s)

Use a library and find the section which contains your subject. If you are not used to using libraries, the staff there will be happy to help you – it's part of their job. Pick out a few books which look as if they might be useful.

2. Check that it's worth reading

Some students call this part 'giving the books the once-over'. It is really a case of checking on whether the book is up to date (look on the back of the title page for the year it was published), written by someone who knows about the subject, is clear and easy to read, has useful illustrations, has an index to help find the parts you need and anything else you want from it.

It should take only a couple of minutes to do this. This is *skim*-reading.

3. Read only the parts you need

When you have decided that the book (or other reading matter) is worth reading, you need to decide which parts you want to read. You may want to read the whole book, or you may just need bits of it. When we read for study we need to be able to select our reading; there is not usually time to read everything.

The parts we decide to read need to be read *carefully*. You may remember from Reading skills that this is the slower method of reading where understanding and remembering is important. We also need to think about what we read and ask ourselves questions about it. Do I agree? What have they missed out? Does it link with other things I've read? Is it fact or just someone's opinion?

4. Make good notes of what you read

Unless you have a remarkable memory, you will need to make notes on what you've read. The section on Notes on p.50 explains the usefulness of notes in study.

When you make notes, use chapter headings and side headings from the book. Try reading the first and last sentences of a paragraph or a chapter again – they are often a good summary.

5. Keep a record of the book(s) you use

Before you put the book back on the shelf, it is important to jot down some details about the book in case you ever need to read it again. Most students should keep a list of books they have used (even if they haven't read the whole book).

A list of books used in study is called a *bibliography*.

REMEMBER You don't need to buy expensive books for study. You can borrow them from libraries and then you can use them and return them as often as you like.

ASSIGNMENT Visit your local library with a subject in mind. It should be something that you are interested in or are studying for now.

Find the section in the library which deals with your subject. If you are not sure about how the books are organised, ask the librarian to help you. Librarians are usually keen to help people who want to use the library.

Take a few books about your subject (2 – 3, or more if you like) and give them 'the once-over', using the following checklist. Or, better still, make your own.

Questions to ask about the book
When was it written – is it up to date?
Who wrote it – are they qualified on the subject?
Is there an index at the back?
Is there a contents page?
Are there useful diagrams or pictures?
Is there a useful introduction?
Does it look readable to you?

After a while you'll be able to carry your checklist in your head.

Now choose which you think is the best book on the subject. For this assignment just choose one, although you would normally make notes on several books if they all seemed useful. Use the book to *read carefully* and make good *notes* on the parts that you think are worth recording. (See p.50.)

If you are making very brief notes, you may find it useful to use a plain postcard. You can put your notes on one side and use the other side to record the details of the book.

You can buy small index cards in a box if you are really thinking of studying and using notes regularly or you could make your own.

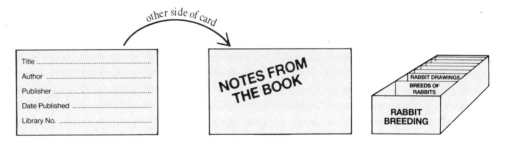

Think about the things that make up good study reading. Which of them are likely to help *you* with your study reading?

	✓
Using different reading methods – **skim, scan, light, careful**	
Using the library more often	
Using the 5 steps to read for study	
Making notes and keeping details of books read	

Anyone can study – you don't need to be a student at college. If you are interested in learning more about anything at all, then by reading and researching the subject you are *studying*.

Reading for pleasure

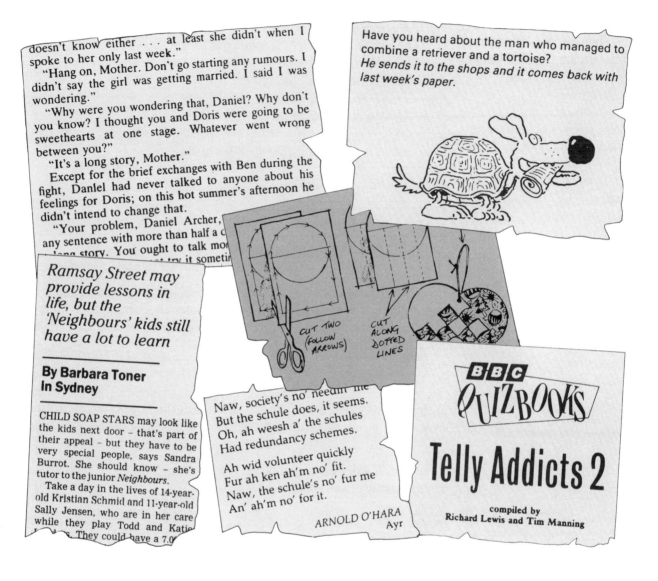

doesn't know either . . . at least she didn't when I spoke to her only last week."

"Hang on, Mother. Don't go starting any rumours. I didn't say the girl was getting married. I said I was wondering."

"Why were you wondering that, Daniel? Why don't you know? I thought you and Doris were going to be sweethearts at one stage. Whatever went wrong between you?"

"It's a long story, Mother."

Except for the brief exchanges with Ben during the fight, Daniel had never talked to anyone about his feelings for Doris; on this hot summer's afternoon he didn't intend to change that.

"Your problem, Daniel Archer, any sentence with more than half a ~~long story. You ought to talk mo~~

Ramsay Street may provide lessons in life, but the 'Neighbours' kids still have a lot to learn

By Barbara Toner In Sydney

CHILD SOAP STARS may look like the kids next door – that's part of their appeal – but they have to be very special people, says Sandra Burrot. She should know – she's tutor to the junior *Neighbours*.

Take a day in the lives of 14-year-old Kristian Schmid and 11-year-old Sally Jensen, who are in her care while they play Todd and Katie. They could have a 7.0

Have you heard about the man who managed to combine a retriever and a tortoise?
He sends it to the shops and it comes back with last week's paper.

CUT TWO (FOLLOW ARROWS)

CUT ALONG DOTTED LINES

Naw, society's no' needin' me
But the schule does, it seems.
Oh, ah weesh a' the schules
Had redundancy schemes.

Ah wid volunteer quickly
Fur ah ken ah'm no' fit.
Naw, the schule's no' fur me
An' ah'm no' for it.

ARNOLD O'HARA
Ayr

BBC QUIZBOOKS

Telly Addicts 2

compiled by
Richard Lewis and Tim Manning

Reading for pleasure is all about | choice | and | freedom. |

We have a | choice | of *what* we read and *how* we read it.

We have the | freedom | to read *when* we like and *where* we like.

Most reading for pleasure is *light reading* (see p. 57). It shouldn't be boring or feel like hard work. If you read any of the following for pleasure whenever you want to, you may just want to *skim* through the rest of this section. If you never read for pleasure or think you would like to do more, this section may interest you.

Reading for pleasure includes

- ☑ magazines
- ☑ newspapers
- ☑ jokes
- ☑ poems

- ☑ novels (fiction)
- ☑ short stories
- ☑ information books (non-fiction)
- ☑ life stories – biographies, autobiographies

Choices in reading

Magazines and newspapers

It's really up to you *what* you read, *how much* of it you read and whether you read it *quickly* or *slowly*. Very few people read everything in magazines or newspapers.

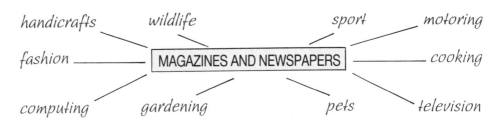

So be choosy – flick through and find something interesting; read *lightly* and if you change your mind or find it heavy going, leave it and don't feel bad about finding something else to read.

Novels, short stories, poems and information books

Some people like to own books. They have favourites which they read again and again. Others prefer to borrow books from a library. Many do both.

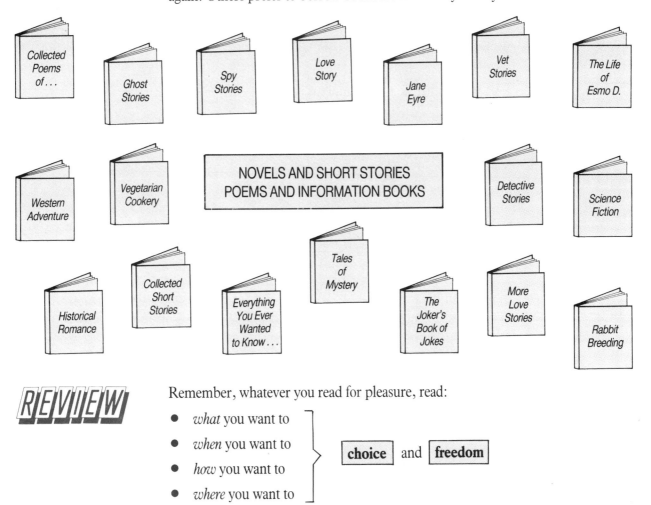

REVIEW

Remember, whatever you read for pleasure, read:

- *what* you want to
- *when* you want to
- *how* you want to
- *where* you want to

choice and freedom

3. Talking and listening

> . . . and then the man in the blue suit, who'd been standing near the back, well, he stood up and walked right up to . . .

Most of us learn to **talk** quite early on in life. We soon take it for granted as something we can do.

Most of us think we know how to **listen**. We listen to thousands of things in as many different ways . . .

- to the boss giving orders
- to music
- to kettles boiling
- to the radio
- to people at meetings
- to lecturers lecturing
- to babies crying
- to sales people selling
- to telephones ringing
- to an angry neighbour
- to tales of woe
- TV
- to children after school
- to friends talking

NOTE

- Neither skill is as simple as it might seem.
- Both need developing for use in different situations.
- Neither are just about words.

When do we talk?

In different roles
- as a parent
- as a spouse
- as a child
- as a friend
- as a boss
- as a learner
- as a leader

General conversation

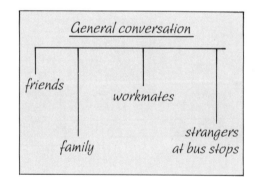

friends
workmates
family
strangers
at bus stops

At work
- to customers
- with colleagues
- with the boss
- to people on the phone

For you to add your own

In a group
- at the pub
- at a union meeting
- at evening class
- at the club

In particular situations
- as father of the bride
- at the doctor's
- in shops
- to teachers at parents' evenings
- to advise others

How do we talk?

We use different kinds of language for different situations; some talking is spontaneous and fairly unthought out; some we plan out in advance. Some people love talking . . . others avoid it whenever possible.

> Sometimes we don't know what we *think* until we *hear* ourselves say it.

We talk to people   at people   **with** people

People who talk at you are mainly listening to themselves. They are not really looking for or waiting for a response from their listeners. They just need an audience.

People who talk with you welcome your involvement in the process.

People who talk to you have usually taken you into account before they start and care about how you are responding to what they have to say.

Think

Do you tend to talk mostly **with, to** or **at** people?

Do you need to think about this some more?

Talking and communication

Talking that is part of a real attempt to communicate with others has *purpose*. It hopes to achieve particular things and to take those on the receiving end properly into account.

Talking as a means of communication is more than words – it involves the whole person. Many extra messages are signalled when someone is talking by . . .

whether they look at you directly

whether they smile . . . sometimes

how closely they stand or lean towards you

what they are wearing

whether they close their eyes

the way they sit or stand

the way they use their face

whether they sit with tightly folded arms

the way they use their hands

whether they shout a lot or speak very quietly

whether they stumble over words and leave too many silences

whether they rattle on regardless

More than words

These messages without words are called

| BODY LANGUAGE | or | NON–VERBAL COMMUNICATION |

If ever you see a profoundly deaf person using Sign Language you will really see body language in action! It involves:

facial expressions   *gestures*   *body positions*   *eyebrows*   *eye movements*

Listening and communication

All the body language signals mentioned as part of *talking* can also tell you a great deal about how well someone is *listening* to you and a lot of what they feel about what you are saying.

Now think about yourself in different talking situations:

> How do *you* listen?
>
> How do you sit, stand, hold your arms, focus your eyes?
>
> How quickly, slowly, loudly do you speak?
>
> Do you fill in any silences as quickly as they arise?

> Do you think you are a good listener? Why?
>
> Do you think you are a good communicator? Why?

> Next time you are on the telephone or listening to the radio, think about what's missing compared to when you are talking face to face with someone.
>
> How do you compensate?
>
> Is it harder work? Why?

Questions

Questions are a major part of talking and listening skills. There are different kinds of questions. You should be aware of this both for when you are asking and when you are answering them.

Some questions are closed

Closed questions suggest there is only one correct answer (usually 'yes' or 'no'), that the speaker has it and can you guess what it is. This form of question is self-limiting. It is good if you are conducting a quiz or checking back a detail you've just communicated or had communicated to you.

e.g. 'If I move this lever, will the safety barrier rise?'

Some questions are rhetorical

A rhetorical question does not really require you to answer at all!

e.g. 'Do we really want the Morden Engineering Plant to close down, brothers?'

Some questions are open

Open questions involve the listener. They ask the listener to think and respond using their own experience and reactions.

e.g. 'What do you think about closing down the Morden Engineering Plant?'

Here the communication is two-way.

It can be hard to ask questions

Sometimes you may feel you can't ask a question because you are embarrassed, don't want to look stupid, not sure of the right question to ask or actually afraid of the person you should be asking. Such feelings could interfere with communication and cause misunderstandings.

Do you often have such feelings yourself? Are you good at asking questions? Are you good at answering questions?

Questions can guide a conversation. Look at the questions in this dialogue. See how they help both the customer and the management to get what they need.

Hello. May I help you?
Hmm. Yes, I'd like to book a table.

When would you like it for?
Oh! Tonight please.

Is that for two people or more?
Just two people . . . and not too late.

What time would suit you?
8.30 would be OK.

8.30? Fine. Would you prefer upstairs or downstairs, non-smoking or the subdued lighting area?
No. Anywhere will do.

Thank you. That's nearly all. Could I just have your name and address please?

Making your point

Making your point is not always easy to do! It's often hard to be sure you've made it successfully and it's not always accepted even when you have done so . . .

Helpful hints

- Make your point because you are *convinced* of it.
- *Think* about your main point beforehand.
- Make some *notes* if it helps.
- *Practise* on friends first if you like.

- *Support* your opinions with specific points and information.
- Take your *time.*
- *Involve* your listener.
- Check back and *clarify* points with your listener as you go along.
- *Keep cool!* Your point may be valid, well argued, very reasonable . . . but still not accepted! Sorry. That's life.

Giving instructions

This kind of communication usually benefits from plenty of thought and experience. It may often require you to use very precise or specialist language.

Try describing the picture below to someone else so that they can make an exact copy from the information you give them.

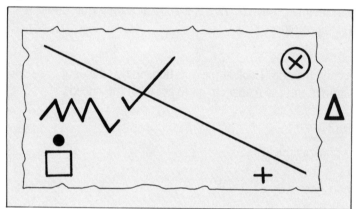

But . . .

The person receiving the words and instructions from you isn't allowed to speak at all and you must do the exercise with your backs to one another . . . or with each of you out of sight of the other. However you do it, there is to be no communication except by words from you!

Write down a few of the things that this last activity highlighted for you about communicating effectively with another person. Ask the person you worked with for some of their reactions too.

If you are *listening* to instructions you must ask for clarification, especially of unfamiliar words. Ask for the words to be repeated if you don't get something the first time. Be an active, responsible listener.

The sound of your voice

Many people have voices and ways of talking that are really enjoyable to listen to. In showbusiness lots of people do voiceovers for adverts because their voices appeal to listeners; they sell the products!

When someone whose voice you like talks to you or you hear them speaking, try to analyse what it is about the way they speak and sound that appeals to you.

Tick the things that matter to you. Add others if you wish.

easy on the ear		softly spoken		fluency	
clear speech		not squeaky			
slow/but not too slow		has authority			
husky		not all on one note			
has an accent		has a laugh in it			

Look at the things you have ticked or added. Why did you choose these things? Do any of them feature in your own voice or speaking style? Would you like them to? Could you add some of this variety into your own style?

Pronunciation

Accents can make a speaking voice very attractive or interesting. They can also interfere with communication if they are very strong and hard to understand. Think about Russ Abbott's Glaswegian character, Jimmy McJimmy, or Oz in *Auf Wiedersehen Pet*, or Marlon Brando in *The Godfather*.

Today, both in radio and on television, you will hear a much wider range of accents than you would have done 20 years ago. For example, the current Blue Peter presenters feature one definite Northern accent, an Irish brogue, and a fairly strong Scottish accent. And what about Patti Coldwell's Lancashire sounds? . . . And Derek Jameson's gravelly, cockney tones?

Mind you . . . when it comes to reading the news things haven't changed a lot!

What do you think the Broadcasting Authorities look for in their news presenters in terms of their voice and speaking skills? Make a list of your ideas.

Being judged by your voice

The sound of a voice and the way a person speaks may affect the way they are listened to and how seriously what they say is taken. This is not necessarily fair or very scientific, but it does still seem to be the case to some degree.

What do you think about this?

ON TELEVISION recently it was reported that many Manchester business men were starting elocution lessons as they felt their Northern accents were holding them back when they were dealing with their Southern colleagues and counterparts.

But

On the other hand there have been very many successful Northern business men . . . and women, and many other successful people with regional accents in all walks of life. So there must be more to effective talking than the way you pronounce your vowel sounds!

And there is . . .

Talking and listening go together. They are about interacting with other people to get messages across, exchange ideas, give instructions, learn about each other.

- Both are responsibilities.

- Both are skilled forms of communication.

- Both can be developed and improved through increased awareness and practice.

Here are some general pointers about talking that you might like to bear in mind.

Tips for talkers

- Be aware of who you are talking to and why.

- Be aware of whether you are at ease or uncomfortable and why.

- Take the listener into account. You are not talking to yourself!

- Be aware of your own body language or other speech habits. Do you rub your nose a lot? Do you have pet phrases like 'to be perfectly honest . . .'?

- Try not to cover your mouth or chew a pencil whilst you talk. Some listeners lip-read as well as listen to the sounds.

- Watch out for the signals coming from your listener and take notice of them.

- Check your listener's understanding from time to time by asking confirming questions or answering theirs.

- You may sometimes need to plan what you want to say in advance, writing notes if necessary.

- Don't be afraid of reasonable silences. These are a necessary and natural part of talking and listening.

Tips for listeners

> Listening can be a form of counselling. Perhaps someone needs to share a problem, talk about their grief or test out a great idea on you.
>
> **OR**
>
> Listening can be a straightforward part of a two-way communication process involving information exchange, instructions, arguing a point, learning something new, etc.

The following tips may vary according to the situation you are in.

- Listening means giving time . . . so make some.

- Listening is not just about hearing; it's about making sense of what's being said.

- Listening is active, not passive. You may be sitting still, but you *are* involved.

- Even if you are not expected to say a lot, indicate your involvement with nods and smiles and encouraging sounds and words.

- Take into account the speaker's tone of voice and other non-verbal signals when you are trying to understand their point. Sometimes the spoken words and the body language don't match!

- Try not to be distracted or do things that will distract the speaker.

- Try to see things from the speaker's viewpoint . . . *empathise*.

- Don't just listen out for key words or phrases. Try to get the whole picture, otherwise you will stop listening and start looking for spaces to push in your own reactions to unconnected details.

- *Don't* interrupt unnecessarily, but *do* ask for clarification when you need it.

- Don't automatically fill silences. They are part of the communication process.

Books

There are many books about 'talking' and 'listening' especially related to counselling. Most are quite heavy going. There are some books on communication with a few pages on 'talking' and 'listening'. It's probably best if you ask at your local library for help in finding something.

Increase your awareness. Think about and discuss with others the

talking and listening skills in these situations:

A visit to the doctor's with an illness

Talking to the childminder you may ask to take care of your 2-year-old

Visiting a friend in hospital

Asking the bank for a large overdraft

Talking to a very deaf old lady

As a supervisor, having to discipline a bad timekeeper

Attending a parents evening at your child's school

Giving a speech at a wedding or a farewell party

Talking to a child lost on a day out at Woburn Abbey

Jury service

Talking to someone who has recently lost a close relative

Taking part in a meeting to decide on who to elect as Club President

Talking to a telephone salesperson

Using the telephone

This section looks at using the telephone to get things done at work or at home.

Some people love using the telephone and, even at work, spend a long time over calls.

Other people hate the phone and dread using it.

Whether we like it or not, most of us have to use the phone sometimes. Our calls could be for a variety of reasons:

to arrange things

to pass on information

to complain

to give information

to ask for information

to buy

to reassure

to give your opinion

Here are some of the answers people often give when asked why they don't like using the telephone:

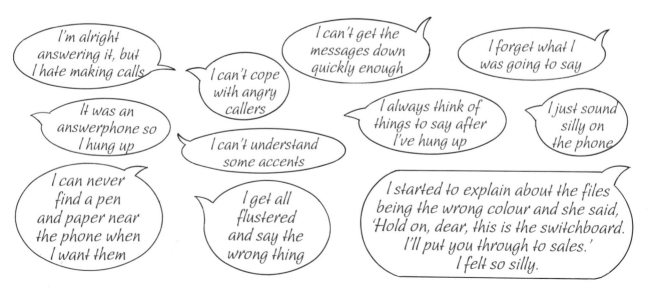

I'm alright answering it, but I hate making calls

I can't cope with angry callers

I can't get the messages down quickly enough

I forget what I was going to say

It was an answerphone so I hung up

I can't understand some accents

I always think of things to say after I've hung up

I just sound silly on the phone

I can never find a pen and paper near the phone when I want them

I get all flustered and say the wrong thing

I started to explain about the files being the wrong colour and she said, 'Hold on, dear, this is the switchboard. I'll put you through to sales.' I felt so silly.

These comments show the 2 main reasons why some people are not effective on the telephone:

- lack of confidence
- lack of preparation

If you are not | **prepared** | you may not feel | **confident** |

But

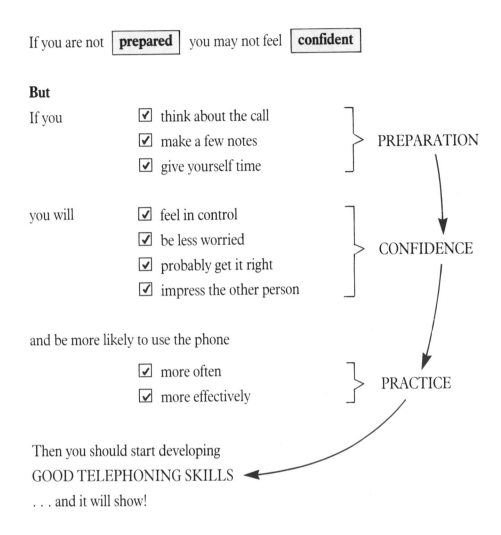

If you
- ☑ think about the call
- ☑ make a few notes
- ☑ give yourself time

PREPARATION

you will
- ☑ feel in control
- ☑ be less worried
- ☑ probably get it right
- ☑ impress the other person

CONFIDENCE

and be more likely to use the phone
- ☑ more often
- ☑ more effectively

PRACTICE

Then you should start developing
GOOD TELEPHONING SKILLS
. . . and it will show!

Preparing to make a call

Some calls are easy and do not need much planning:

> Jo, can you bring a copy of the Safety Report to the meeting

> I'll be half an hour late . . .

> Can I book a table for 4 people for 12.30 today please?

However, some calls may be difficult or too important to risk getting things wrong. For example:

| making a complaint | | ordering goods | | collecting information |

If the call needs more thought and planning, you should think about several things.

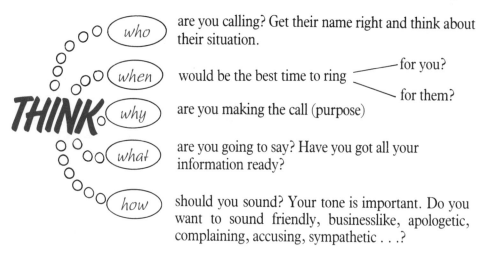

who are you calling? Get their name right and think about their situation.

when would be the best time to ring — for you? / for them?

why are you making the call (purpose)

what are you going to say? Have you got all your information ready?

how should you sound? Your tone is important. Do you want to sound friendly, businesslike, apologetic, complaining, accusing, sympathetic . . .?

You should always aim to sound polite; it rarely pays to be rude on the phone.

Make a few notes

It often helps to jot down a few notes and have them beside you when you phone. It's easy to forget things.

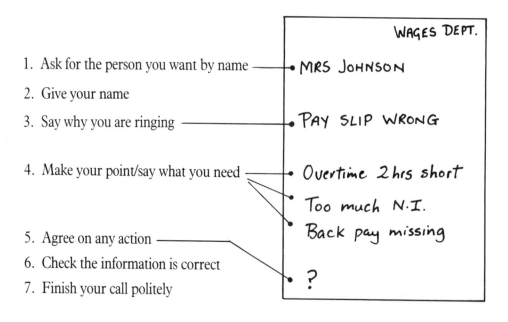

1. Ask for the person you want by name —— MRS JOHNSON (WAGES DEPT.)

2. Give your name

3. Say why you are ringing —— PAY SLIP WRONG

4. Make your point/say what you need —— Overtime 2 hrs short / Too much N.I. / Back pay missing

5. Agree on any action —

6. Check the information is correct

7. Finish your call politely —— ?

Telephone nerves

Some people do all the things listed on this page and the telephone call is still difficult because they get nervous and flustered. If this happens to you, it really isn't very comforting to know that other people suffer too. You need a way to cope or to get rid of the nervousness.

You may find the following simple tips useful:

- Breathe deeply 3 times before you answer or while you're dialling
- Try to speak slower than usual – we all rush when we're nervous
- Try to lower your voice
- Allow a second or two of silence between sentences

Preparing to take a call

If the caller is as organised as you are then your task of taking the call should be easy.

But not all callers are prepared or confident

And you may be worried about getting the information down quickly enough.

So, it is a good idea to be prepared in the same way as for making a call.

Messages

If you often need to take calls or telephone messages at home or at work, you might find a message pad useful.

Message pads cut down the amount of writing you need to do. They also give you *headings* to remind you what information you need from the caller.

You can buy ready-printed message pads in shops or you could make your own.

Bought

```
Day: _____ Time: ____
Caller: _____
Their no: _____
Message:
```
Homemade

Tip

Use carbon paper to get copies or get someone to photocopy them, four at a time, then cut and staple them together.

REMEMBER

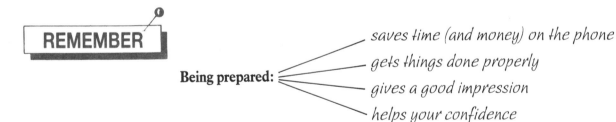

Being prepared:
— saves time (and money) on the phone
— gets things done properly
— gives a good impression
— helps your confidence

This leads to good communication.

Some general tips for telephoning

- always have pen and paper handy
- have any information ready
- check you have the right person
- give your name
- think of the call as a letter with an opening/middle/signing off
- think of the other person's situation
- listen to the tone of their voice. Is it nervous/angry/impatient?
- speak clearly and not too fast. (We notice other people's accents but forget that we may have one too!)
- finish the call politely and clearly

Special tips for using the telephone at work

- answer the phone promptly

- give your name *and* your department

- check that you/they are talking to the right person

- deal with *all* calls politely but briefly (time is money at work)

- offer to ring back if you need to check information

- if you take down information, check that you've done so accurately

- agree the action required by both parties

- finish the call briefly but politely

Coping with the unexpected

Sometimes, even with careful planning, things don't go as expected.

Wrong number, person or department	Always check that you have the right person before you start. If necessary, apologise or ask to be put through to the right person or department.
Cut off during call. You both redial and both get the engaged signal	The person who dialled in the first place is the one responsible for re-dialling.
Caller is difficult to understand	Accents, fast talking and bad lines can be a problem. Try saying 'I'm sorry, it's a bad line, can you speak slowly and clearly'.
Angry person on the phone	The best way to cope with angry calls is to do the opposite. • They shout – you speak softly • They rush – you slow down • They are rude – you are extremely polite It's hard to do, but it usually works!

Answerphones

Most people find answerphones worrying but as they are becoming more popular many of us will have to get used to them.

If you know the person on the answerphone – just try to imagine they are really there, being a very good listener. If you really can't talk, try not to hang up. Say 'Hello, it's .... but I'd rather talk to *you*. I'll ring back later.'

If it's a business line – you should be prepared in your mind or better still on paper, so just read out your message! You can, of course, just leave your name, number and the date and time of your call. Try not just to hang up!

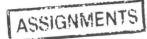

1. Next time you need to make an important call, try making a few notes in preparation.

   Try also to look through the tips to see if there is anything else you could do to improve your communication on the telephone.

2. Think about using a message pad for work or home. Perhaps other people at your workplace or your family would find it helpful.

Think about the **purpose** of the call, the **other person** and their situation.

Look back to the comments on page 78. Use the checklist below to say what you think the problem is and try to think of some advice you would give for each.

The first one is done for you.

Comments from page 78	Lack of confidence	Lack of preparation	Other reason	Advice/suggestions
I forget what I was going to say		✓	possible nerves	Think and prepare before you ring — maybe make a few notes.
I can't understand some accents				
I can't cope with angry callers				
I just sound silly on the phone				
I'm alright answering it but I hate making calls				
I can't get the messages down quickly enough				
I always think of things to say after I've hung up				
I get all flustered and say the wrong thing				
It was an answerphone so I hung up				
I can never find a pen and paper near the phone when I want them				
I started to explain . . . she said 'Hold on, dear, this is the switchboard' . . . I felt so silly				

Communication in groups

What is a group?

A group is more than 2 people gathered together for a *particular purpose*, or involving people with *something in common*.

A group may involve 6 people or 16 people or 66 people.

This section is about some of the ways communication happens in groups.

Different groups

Some groups you are assigned to

| school class | — | family | — | the unemployed |

Some you join

| budgie breeders | — | Neighbourhood Watch | — | Caribbean Club |

Some groups are informal

| down the pub: more of a haphazard gathering |

Some groups are very formal

| Anti-Nuclear Action Group |

Once you have a number of people together then you have:

- a range of experiences
- a variety of preferences for ways of doing things
- different personalities

These factors mean **dynamics**: the **energy** made by **differences** between people all trying to work and communicate within a group.

Communicating within an organised group

How people communicate in a group will depend on many things:

The size of the group: more than 10 people and it will be hard for some to speak out at all.

Leadership: who is in charge. The atmosphere they create. Whether there is a leader at all. Or if it keeps changing.

The rules developed or followed: some groups are very structured with laid down rules and roles for people in the group. These can help if they give people a way of communicating. They can hinder if they get in the way of communication.

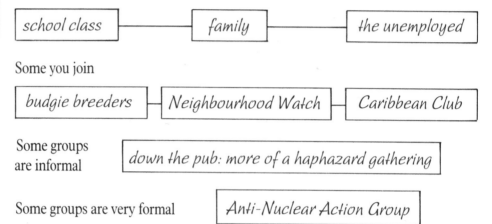

How the seating is arranged: rigid rows stop people from talking and listening to each other easily. A circle could change all that . . . and affect the leadership and the way people see themselves in the group.

Whether the people in the group know each other.

The purpose of the group: if this isn't clear or is not acceptable to some group members then it could affect the group badly.

Discussion in groups

Group discussion can be very valuable, because you can learn from other people's experiences and ways of seeing things. To get the most out of a group it may help to know about the different ways people contribute positively to discussion. Some people find discussion in groups very difficult. Others find it all too easy and hog the show! Perhaps you could start to use some of the following helpful ways yourself.

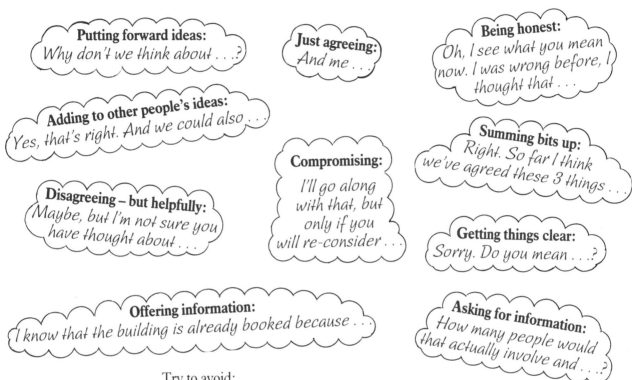

Putting forward ideas:
Why don't we think about . . .?

Just agreeing:
And me . . .

Being honest:
Oh, I see what you mean now. I was wrong before, I thought that . . .

Adding to other people's ideas:
Yes, that's right. And we could also . . .

Compromising:
I'll go along with that, but only if you will re-consider . . .

Summing bits up:
Right. So far I think we've agreed these 3 things . . .

Disagreeing – but helpfully:
Maybe, but I'm not sure you have thought about . . .

Getting things clear:
Sorry. Do you mean . . .?

Offering information:
I know that the building is already booked because . . .

Asking for information:
How many people would that actually involve and . . .?

Try to avoid:

- Nitpicking
- Being plain obstructive
- Dominating the discussion
- Not contributing anything to the discussion

Business meetings

These are often formal with special:

Rules:
Particular ways of doing things, e.g. asking questions only through the chairperson or only being able to vote if certain numbers of people are present at the meeting.

Roles:

The Chairperson: Is in charge of the meeting. Decides who will speak and in what order.	*The Secretary:* Takes the notes. Sends out letters. Organises the agenda.	*Treasurer:* Keeps the accounts. Reports to the meeting.

- At the beginning of such meetings *minutes* may have to be read and agreed: these are a summary of what happened at the last meeting.
- The meeting may follow a tight pattern using an *agenda*. This is a short list of things to be discussed at the meeting.

- You can add extra items under *A.O.B.* (Any Other Business), which will be dealt with at the end of the agenda, or through *matters arising* from the minutes at the start of the meeting.

- Experience will eventually help you communicate more effectively in this sort of group.

In group situations try to use these guidelines:

- *Look* at the person or people you are talking to.

- *Do* make points: they allow others to 'hear' what you think.

- *Allow* others the chance to say what they think too.

- *Encourage* others by valuing any efforts they make to say things.

- *Listen* properly: don't just use the space when others are talking to plan your next contribution.

- *Respond* to what you hear being said.

- *Disagree* if it will broaden the discussion and the point is genuine, but do so reasonably!

- *Support* other people's views if they are also your own, but they got in first.

- *Avoid* aggression. It will make you feel bad; it will make others feel bad; it will not develop the discussion.

- *Ask* for clarification when you don't understand something: chances are others won't have understood either!

- *Learn* about the rules and roles in formal meetings and start using them to advantage.

Interviews

You might be in an interview situation as an *interviewer*.

You might be the person being *interviewed*.

Interviews are two-way communication: *interviewer* and *interviewee* are both trying to find out about each other.

Situations where you might interview or be interviewed include:

finding a babyminder

getting a loan

finding some voluntary work

for a place on a course

renting a flat

for a job

looking for household help

Whatever the reason, whatever part you are playing, the guidelines remain the same. Interviewers are usually looking for signs of:

Reliability   Honesty   Suitability   Potential

Interviewees may need reassurance on these same points.

A job interview

This is the interview most likely to worry people.

The following suggestions might be helpful for job seekers, but they could also be useful in other interview situations too.

Before the interview

Research the job: what does it involve? Does it need someone ... with physical strength? ... good at figures? ... good with machines? ... able to work alone? ... good with people? ... happy with repetition? ... happy indoors? ... happy outdoors? ... able to supervise? ... able to take pressure? ... able to drive? ... etc., etc.

Research the firm or the organisation: what do they do or make? When was it established? How many people work there? What facilities are provided for staff? What is their reputation as employers? Do they encourage career development?

Decide what to wear: this may depend on your circumstances, but bear the job in mind. Don't overdo it. Be comfortable and confident. Perhaps be more than 'everyday' in your choice of clothes, but not overdressed.

Time and place: be sure of when and where the interview is to take place. Check the time. Do you know how to get there? How are you going? Car? Bus? Taxi? On foot? How long will it take to get there? Maybe you need to do a trial run before the interview to be sure of your timing. Punctuality matters.

Paperwork: will you need any certificates, forms or references with you at the interview? If you do, get them all together well in advance of the interview itself.

And think about

> **Questions you might be asked:** why did you apply for the job? What do you think the job involves? What particular strengths do you have to offer this post? Can you work alone? Do you work well with other people? Could you supervise other people? How would you feel about doing overtime or shiftwork? What other work experience have you? What are your hobbies and interests? Do you see yourself progressing in your career? Do you want training opportunities? Have you any health problems? Do you drive? Do you smoke? Do you have any questions for us?

> **Questions you could ask:** many of your questions may be answered during the interview itself: point this out if it is the case. Make a list of possible questions before you go and don't be afraid to refer to it. It will show the care you have taken in preparing for the interview. You might want to ask about pay, holidays, health schemes, clothing and tool allowances, training opportunities, canteen and social facilities . . .

On the day

> **On arriving:** report to reception and explain who you are and why you have come. Use the toilet if you need to. Try to relax: take some deep breaths; think about the things you want to say in the interview; if you feel you have to have a cigarette check whether it's acceptable.

> **At the interview:** you will be being assessed on how you look, how you react, how you conduct yourself, what you say and how you say it. Don't sit down until you are asked or until it makes sense for you to ask where you might sit. Don't smoke or eat at the interview. Sit comfortably, not slouched or bolt upright! Try to keep your hands fairly still. Don't fiddle with jewellery. Look at whoever is talking to you. Listen as hard as you can and try to answer questions in ways that reply to the point, but which also sell yourself well. Answer with more than 'yes' or 'no', but don't go on and on. Speak as clearly as you can. Ask when you are not sure of what is being said or required of you. Make the most of any previous experience you have had. Try to enjoy the interview and be really interested in the whole proceedings.

Afterwards

Throughout the interview try to decide if you really want the job. If you do, and you don't get it, it might be worth ringing up or writing to ask for some 'feedback' that might help you at the next interview.

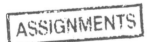

Find an advert for a real job and try preparing for it as suggested above.

Look back at the other interview situations at the start of this section. Choose one and then see how you could use the 'guidelines' for job interviews to prepare successfully for this different kind of interview. Be methodical. Plan out your thinking in a diagram if you wish.

Communicating with graphics

Communicating is all about transmitting (sending) and receiving messages. Graphics are used to send messages *visually* rather than with lines and lines of text. By taking facts and figures that are buried in words and presenting them graphically you can often transmit a lot of information more clearly and quickly.

In the example below a long and repetitive piece of writing is offered in a simple chart called a 'table'. They offer the same information, but quite differently.

This? ⟶ or, this?

WRITTEN

A survey aimed at pinpointing the main activities people engage in on almost a daily basis discovered the following: information: of those involved in the survey some 72% watched television every day, or almost every day. This activity was the most popular of the ten activities cited. Close on its heels was reading a newspaper, which 70% of those asked carried out on more or less a daily basis. After these two activities the percentage suddenly drops to 46% which was the figure representing those people who listened to music at home. Next came ..... etc ... etc ....

TABLE

WHAT DO YOU DO? Every day, or almost every day, the percentage of people who:		EXERCISE OR JOG **35%**
		SPEND AN EVENING JUST TALKING TO SOMEONE **30%**
WATCH TELEVISION **72%**		READ A BOOK **24%**
READ A NEWSPAPER **70%**		PURSUE A HOBBY **23%**
LISTEN TO MUSIC AT HOME **46%**		WORK IN THE GARDEN **22%**
TALK ON PHONE TO FRIENDS OR RELATIVES **45%**		ENGAGE IN SEXUAL ACTIVITIES **11%**

REMEMBER

Communicating with graphics involves using few (or no) words. The point is put across in other ways. A graphic is designed to get its message across to as wide an audience as possible with as much impact and clarity as its images and organisation on the page will allow.

Charts

Charts are particularly suitable for presenting numbers and statistics clearly.

There are 4 main types:

- the **table** (shown above)
- the **fever chart** or **line graph**
- the **bar chart**
- the **pie chart**.

Share Prices

pence

T.L.K. Holdings Ltd

400 / 300 / 200 / 100 / 0

1984 85 86 87 88

Fever chart: named after the one on the end of the hospital bed!

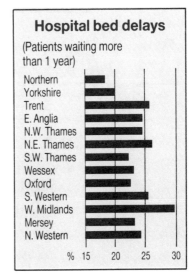

Hospital bed delays

(Patients waiting more than 1 year)

Northern / Yorkshire / Trent / E. Anglia / N.W. Thames / N.E. Thames / S.W. Thames / Wessex / Oxford / S. Western / W. Midlands / Mersey / N. Western

% 15 20 25 30

Bar chart: The columns can be vertical or horizontal according to the purpose and kind of information being presented.

Pie chart: The information is worked out in percentages and presented as sections of a circle, like pieces of pie.

This pie chart was designed to show people's use of computers at home and at work.

- If you decide to use a chart to present information, choose the kind that you feel will give the clearest picture of what the statistics mean.

- Nowadays, computers, given the right data, will produce wonderful charts and diagrams. Don't be afraid to explore these push-button possibilities.

Posters and notices

Notices and posters are usually skimmed quickly, so in designing them your main aims will be:

- to catch attention

- to make sure all the information you want people to have is there and as easy as possible to get at.

Some useful tips when designing a notice or poster:

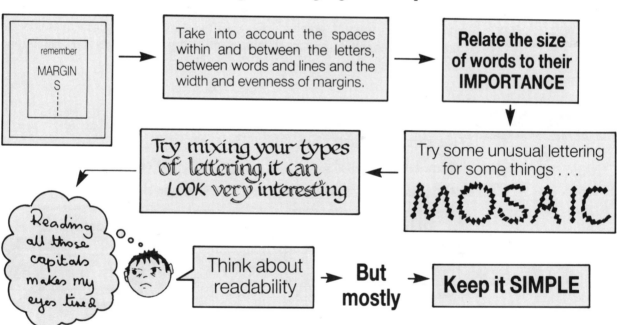

AND

- Consider how you will catch attention: Colour? Pictures? Content? Positioning? Size? Humour? Impact?

- Don't forget about our friend the computer: fancy lettering and graphics are possible in all sizes.

- Photocopy things. Cut out letters from newspapers and magazines. Lick and stick!

- Ensure TIMES . . . DATES . . . PLACES . . . are clear.

- Remember to include contact points. Put phone numbers and names at the bottom.

 Which is the most effective notice . . . and why?

NOTICE TO ALL EMPLOYEES

THE OFFICE PARTY WILL START AT 6pm AND WILL BE HELD ON FRIDAY JUNE 30th IN ROOM 26, MR PARSONS' SECTION ON FLOOR 3.

 At work cluttered noticeboards full of useless or dated information will not communicate effectively with others.

- **Clear them regularly**
- **Organise notices thoughtfully**

Other types of graphics

Our daily life is full of messages communicated through graphics. Most we read and interpret without a second thought.

 Which graphics forms in the following list are you aware of? See if you can match some with the actual examples given below.

> *Timetables   Rotas   Schedules   Warning signs   Badges*
> *Highway Code signs   Traffic lights   Zodiac signs   Maps*
> *Signs around town   Brands   Flags   Plans   Designs*
> *Propaganda   Signs & Symbols   X-rays and scans   Logos*
> *Information signs   Cartoons and comic strips   Posters*
> *Labels and Packaging   Pictures   Photos   Diagrams*
> *Whole environments   Instructions   Street murals   Advertising*
> *Computer graphics*

Many exams, tests and work places use charts and statistics. Thanks to the speed at which computers can produce charts, diagrams and pictures, all these forms of graphics are being used increasingly in newspapers, magazines, advertising, books and leaflets.

So . . .

Question: Is using and responding to graphic messages important?

Answer: Yes! Quite definitely. They are all round you. They widen your perceptions and if you use them well yourself you increase the number of people you might affect by your ideas.

- Graphics cut across many barriers, especially those of language.
- Graphics encourage people to read things they might otherwise ignore.
- Graphics greatly increase the scope and impact of communication.
- Graphics can say a lot in a small space.

1. Look at the way symbols and graphics are used in this book, in your newspaper, at work, in town, on TV. Increase your awareness of how, why, when and where they are used.

2. Next time you have information to present think how you might make it more graphical.

3. Design a poster for either a real or made-up purpose.

Designers' Guide to Creating Charts and Diagrams, Nigel Holmes (Watson-Guptill, New York).

Graphic Communication, John Twyford (Batsford Academic & Educational Ltd.).

Communication and IT

What is IT?

IT stands for **Information Technology.**

It is the handling of information by electronic methods and is especially good for storing, sorting, calculating, selecting, changing, sending and displaying information very quickly.

Some people think IT means being taken over by computers. In fact IT is much more than just computers and most of us benefit from its many uses. Even if we never use or even see a computer, we are all involved in this new technology as we go about our daily lives.

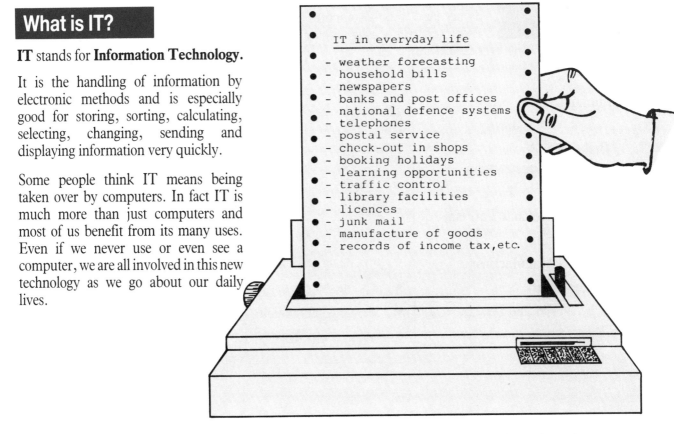

```
IT in everyday life
 - weather forecasting
 - household bills
 - newspapers
 - banks and post offices
 - national defence systems
 - telephones
 - postal service
 - check-out in shops
 - booking holidays
 - learning opportunities
 - traffic control
 - library facilities
 - licences
 - junk mail
 - manufacture of goods
 - records of income tax,etc.
```

Remember, as with all communication, it is important to think about the **purpose** and the **audience.** New technology can often improve communication but sometimes a more traditional method can be a better way to get your message across.

Examples of new technology in everyday life

BOOKING A HOLIDAY

Whether you book your holiday by telephone or visit a travel agency, it is likely that the details will be fed into a computer. The computer will give information about available dates, prices etc., and in some travel agencies the computer can also show you pictures of the resort on the screen. (Videotex).

EASING DISABILITY

IT can make life easier for people who have problems with sight, hearing, speech or movement. Computers can produce speech, braille print-outs, control the opening of doors, heating adjustments in the house and even order your shopping from a local supermarket (and pay for it directly if you have a bank account). There are many other uses of IT which make life easier for people with specific problems and, no doubt, many more being developed for the future.

EQUIPMENT IN THE HOME

Many electrical goods in the home use new technology. There are washing machines, stereos, telephones, microwaves, televisions and videos, all able to be programmed to do just what we want them to.

CAR DRIVERS

All car owners have the details of their cars held on computer. This means that reminders for car tax, police checks (stolen cars, accidents, driving offences, etc) and other information can be handled quickly and efficiently from any police or official computer in the country.

DATA PROTECTION ACT

Many organisations keep records about people on computers. This can sometimes be helpful, as in health care and crime-fighting. But many of us worry about the information (data) being wrong or misused. The Data Protection Act gives the public the right to know and check the correctness of information about them held on computer.

There are useful free leaflets on this subject, available from your local Citizens Advice Bureau or from the following address:

Data Protection Registrar,
Springfield House,
Water Lane,
Wilmslow,
Cheshire SK9 5AX.

Information Technology at work

Many work places use new technology and many more are preparing to do so. Whether you are in work or looking for a job, it is likely that your chances of success in the future will depend on your awareness of the many uses of new technology. You do not need to be a computer expert; just take an interest in new developments. Employers will usually employ, and offer the necessary training to, staff who are keen to learn.

Administration

Catering

Building and Construction

Retail

Travel and Tourism

Hairdressing

Manufacturing

Medical Work

Art and Design

Business Studies

IT provides quick and efficient ways of:

- storing
- sorting
- calculating
- producing text
- producing graphics
- sending information
- receiving information
- linking with others

Car Mechanics

Transport

Journalism

Supermarkets

Armed Services

Banking

Libraries

Farming

Radio and TV Broadcasting

Information Technology in the work place

Wordprocessing

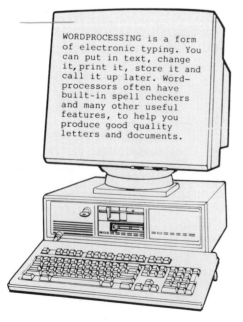

WORDPROCESSING is a form of electronic typing. You can put in text, change it, print it, store it and call it up later. Word-processors often have built-in spell checkers and many other useful features, to help you produce good quality letters and documents.

Databases

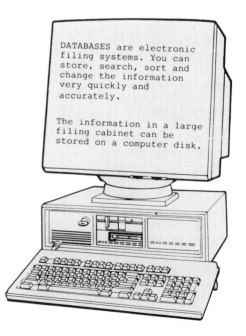

DATABASES are electronic filing systems. You can store, search, sort and change the information very quickly and accurately.

The information in a large filing cabinet can be stored on a computer disk.

Computer Networking

Computer Networking is where several computers are linked, either within the same building or between different sites, often miles apart. The link allows everyone to have access to the same information and to enter or change it so keeping everyone instantly up to date.

Fax machines

Fax (short for facsimile = exact copy) is a way of sending pages of information, both text and graphics, down a telephone line by using electronic coding. It can be expensive but is excellent for sending copies of urgent information instantly.

Computerised photocopies

Some photocopiers can do a range of complicated tasks. You can program them to enlarge, reduce, use different coloured paper, bind, staple sheets together.

Calculation packages

These can do complicated calculations for accounts, wages, profit and loss and many other number-based tasks. They are fast, accurate and easily adapted if the numbers need changing, for example if there is a wage increase or if the product price changes.

Desk Top Publishing (DTP)

These are programs to give good quality visual material which can be designed on the screen and stored or printed in different ways. Some organisations produce their own advertising and other graphical material using DTP.

Prestel

Prestel is British Telecom's database of information which is used by many companies and some private users. With a television set and adaptor you have access to a wide range of subjects and work-related information.

These are just a few of the many uses of IT at work. If you are interested in finding out more, you may like to find the IT section in your library. The books listed at the end of this section are very readable.

Information Technology and study

People sometimes think of learning as being about classrooms, books and teachers. Some of us may remember slates and chalk as being the tools of study! Today there are many exciting ways of learning, whatever your age. Computers are providing people with choices of learning methods. New technology is not taking over; it is giving the learner more power, choice and control in the learning process.

Far from being the master and taking over, computers are here to **slave** for us. We become the **master** in the learning process.

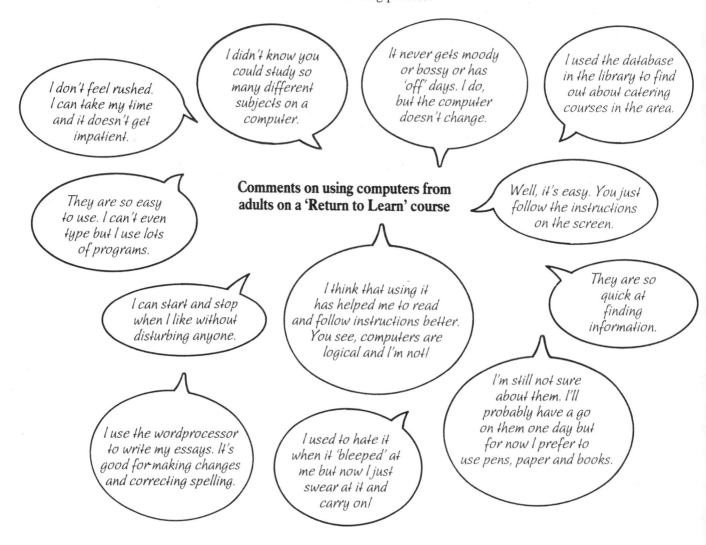

Comments on using computers from adults on a 'Return to Learn' course

I don't feel rushed. I can take my time and it doesn't get impatient.

I didn't know you could study so many different subjects on a computer.

It never gets moody or bossy or has 'off' days. I do, but the computer doesn't change.

I used the database in the library to find out about catering courses in the area.

They are so easy to use. I can't even type but I use lots of programs.

Well, it's easy. You just follow the instructions on the screen.

I can start and stop when I like without disturbing anyone.

I think that using it has helped me to read and follow instructions better. You see, computers are logical and I'm not!

They are so quick at finding information.

I use the wordprocessor to write my essays. It's good for making changes and correcting spelling.

I used to hate it when it 'bleeped' at me but now I just swear at it and carry on!

I'm still not sure about them. I'll probably have a go on them one day but for now I prefer to use pens, paper and books.

Adult learning centres, colleges and, more recently, Opening Learning Centres are providing students with the choice of using IT resources alongside other methods of learning. As one student said, 'It's just another tool for learning, but a very useful one'. IT can help you study at any level and for a wide range of subjects, including basic English and Maths. There are computer programmes which can teach you or help you to assess your own progress and wordprocessors to help you with writing tasks. There are many other IT applications which provide exciting ways of finding, storing, changing and printing information.

If you are interested in finding out more about Information Technology, the books listed below are short, easy-to-read and interesting.

Books

Information Technology – your introductory facts guide (Careers and Occupational Information Centre, 1984).

Living with Computers, I. & R. Cretchley (John Murray, 1985).